The Restaurant
at the Beginning of
the Universe

The Restaurant at the Beginning of the Universe

Exploring the Wonderment of the World through Physics

Anthony P. Pitucco and Shawn Agut

Zephyr
Press®

REACHING THEIR HIGHEST POTENTIAL
TUCSON, ARIZONA

The Restaurant at the Beginning of the Universe
Exploring the Wonderment of the World through Physics

Grades 5–12

©1997 by Zephyr Press
Printed in the United States of America

ISBN 1-56976-056-X

Editors: Stacey Shropshire and Sonya Manes
Cover design: Stirling Crebbs
Design and Production: Daniel Miedaner
Typesetting: Daniel Miedaner

Zephyr Press
P.O. Box 66006
Tucson, AZ 85728-6006

Library of Congress Cataloging-in-Publication Data
Pitucco, Anthony P., 1948-
    The restaurant at the beginning of the universe : exploring the
wonderment of the world through physics / Anthony P. Pitucco and
Shawn Agut.
        p. cm.
    Includes bibliographical referecnes.
    ISBN 1-56976-056-X
    1. Physics—Juvenile literature.   I. Agut, Shawn, 1967-
II. Title.
QC25.P53 1996
530—dc20   96-28581

Anthony Pitucco can be reached at the following e-mail address:
apitucco@pimacc.pima.edu

Contents

Introduction to the Teacher

Welcome to the world of physics and to the exploration of our universe!

As a physics teacher for a number of years, I have learned that the most misunderstood science is physics. It has generally been associated with a high degree of complexity and mathematical mystery. However, the study of the world through the eyes of a physicist actually begins with the beauty of questioning and wonderment. Although the answers that one seeks can lead to complex ideas that *do* require abstract mathematical thought, the initial stages of this process are very simple and very exciting. It was this excitement that propelled me at an early age to pursue science as a career. This pursuit amazed me because in grade school, much to my embarrassment, I could barely do arithmetic.

I realized early on that the passion to learn and to understand had no real boundaries. My simple childhood questions and ideas instilled in me this unparalleled passion, which I hope to unlock in the minds of your students.

Many young adults' perceptions and conceptions about science are locked into a mental framework based upon early educational experiences (some good, some not so good), which may limit their full potential as critical thinkers. To unlock that potential and to tap their childhood passion to learn becomes a challenge; answering that challenge is the purpose of this book.

Be sure to convey to your students all the information in your sections of the book. You may also want to make one copy for each student of the physics newspaper, *Cafe Universe Times,* in the back of the book. The newspaper reviews some of the material in the book in an interesting way and offers students additional activities.

The book is organized around a set of simple observational activities that stimulate questioning and answering. The activities encourage generating answers to stimulate individual creativity. This approach allows young thinkers the flexibility to make mistakes and make misjudgments, and thus necessitates reexamination of the problem. Through these observational activities, a process develops by which students observe, become part of the observation, formulate explanations, develop a language to discuss their ideas, formulate explanations against additional experiments, and encourage active discussions with peers, all of which become the heart of critical analysis.

This process crosses all academic disciplines and is certainly not limited to the sciences, as is evidenced by how we learn to appreciate great masterpieces in literature, art, and music. To compartmentalize science as distinct from other academic studies is a mistake. An even flow among disciplines should exist so that all students understand and appreciate the art of science and the science of science.

If we boil away all the fat, what remains is the true essence of the matter; I believe this book is fat free. Without further ado, turn the page for your first sample from the healthiest menu in the cosmos!

Educational Objectives

- To motivate students who are not necessarily attracted to science and mathematics. Throughout the book, observational activities that integrate drawing, counting, measuring, predicting, recording, hypothesizing, and verifying are used. These activities establish the language of science.

- To develop and sharpen the students' ability to think critically by encouraging

  questioning

  hypothesizing

  observing

  verifying

  researching

  reexamining

  experimenting

  defending

  exploring

  discussing

- To inspire a sense of questioning and wonderment as the students examine the world that surrounds them.

- To stimulate the students' passion for learning.

Introduction to the Student

Have you ever wondered why? Why do some things fall down while others, such as clouds, don't? Why is the sky blue? Why are there waves in the ocean, but not in a pool? Why do I need to go to school? Have all of your "why's" been answered? Have they been answered to your satisfaction? Small children often ask why many times a day! You could think of a physicist as a child who never had enough questions answered and is still asking why. The goal of physics is to understand why and how things work and to formulate explanations as simply and as clearly as possible. It's about experimenting, finding possible answers, and seeing if other answers might be better.

As you go through this book you will be asked to do experiments designed to make you question, to make you curious, and, of course, to make you think. You will also discover that finding answers is only part of the total scientific process.

Listen to your teacher's instructions and read all student sections, which will help give you a better understanding of the concepts and ideas you will be exploring. The text often introduces certain words as vocabulary builders. You are encouraged to look up in a dictionary those words unfamiliar to you and to record the definitions in your laboratory book (more about your laboratory book later). Also, the footnotes have additional research activities for you. All answers to footnotes are to be recorded in your laboratory book.

Creating Your Laboratory Book

Scientists must keep track of all the neat stuff they do. They have to write down every little detail of their experiments; otherwise, they might forget something important. Before you can become a true scientist you must have your own laboratory book where you can record your experiments.

Begin with a fifty- to hundred-page bound notebook. On the cover, write "My Laboratory Book." Include your name, the month, and the year.

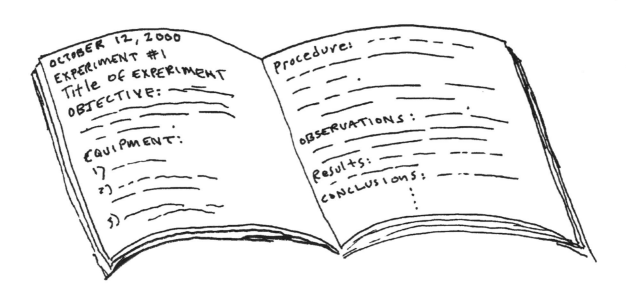

For each activity you perform you will record certain information:

1. date at the top of the page

2. the objective of the experiment

3. the equipment you used

4. the procedure you used for performing the activity or experiment

5. your observations and results

6. your conclusions based on the experiment

7. sketches or diagrams where appropriate

8. answers to all questions that follow each activity and any additional questions your teacher may ask

In addition, set aside two sections for footnote research and word definitions. Your laboratory book is very, very important and should be taken seriously.

Footnote 1

A famous mathematician wrote in the margin of a book he was reading that he had proven (or found the answer to) a very difficult math problem. This problem had puzzled thinkers for centuries and still puzzles them today. The mathematician's last name is Fermat. Go to your library and research him. Write a brief paragraph about him and the famous problem that intrigued him and that he claimed to solve.

Write another paragraph about an inventor from Fermat's historical period and his or her invention.

The Toolbox

You're going to have lots of stuff left over from these experiments. Where are you going to keep it all? In a science toolbox, of course. You can make such a toolbox out of just about anything, so use your imagination. A shoe box will work just fine.

Since we are exploring The Restaurant at the Beginning of the Universe, we should have a menu, so label the side of your toolbox "The Restaurant at the Beginning of the Universe," then label the top of your toolbox "The Menu."

Okay, okay, now let's get on with the good stuff. You have just arrived at a

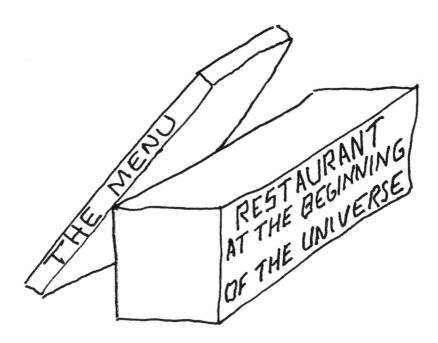

strange and mysterious but wonderful new restaurant. You are really hungry for brain food and all the food that counts! The extraterrestrial maitre d' (a very strange but very calm waiter) greets you at the door and hands you a colorful menu . . .

An Appetizer

Becoming a Physicist

To the Teacher

Objective

Students will formulate questions and analyze the answers to questions.

Equipment

pencil

paper

lots of imagination

Procedure

Divide the class into small groups, with each group discussing a set of questions you have raised, such as those that follow. Have each group select a member as the group physicist who will record all the answers. At the end of the activity, each group physicist will present the group's answers to the class.

Encourage

free thinking

answers suggesting other questions

obvious answers

not-so-obvious answers

rational responses

irrational responses

faulty analogies

Discourage

use of technical language as an end in itself, such as "an object falls because of gravity"

responses that avoid the questions

irrelevant responses

silly responses

1 ◆ An Appetizer

To the Student

Scientists and, in particular, physicists are much like detectives or spies. They generate questions and search to find answers to questions such as "What is . . . ?" "How is . . . ?" and "Why is . . . ?" Finding such answers isn't necessarily easy. When found or proposed, the answers may not be good enough for physicists. Oh, no! They seek answers to help them understand why things work as they do, and they are not satisfied until they can explain it to others clearly. Some individuals, skeptics, don't necessarily believe every answer scientists or physicists suggest. Thus physicists have a heavy burden: they must prove (or show the validity of) every detail, no matter how minute. Until every "What is . . . ?" "How is . . . ?" and "Why is . . . ?" in the universe is answered, there will be scientists and, in particular, physicists.

Your group physicist (you may call her or him the group physicist from now on if you would like to) will pose some questions for you to discuss, such as the ones that follow. You will write down some of your answers, then discuss your answers among your group. Keep writing and discussing until you come to one, two, or three answers to each question that you all agree are possible. When you have finished, the group physicist will write down the agreed-upon answers and present them to the class for discussion.

Questions

1. Why do objects fall to Earth?

2. Do all objects "fall" to Earth?

3. What is the shape of your head?

4. Why is it this shape?

5. Why are some clouds white?

6. Why are other clouds dark?

7. Are all clouds white or dark?

8. Why is the sky blue?

Can you think of some more? Ask a few more questions on your own.

9.

10.

11.

Following are some answers that are not good, and you should be able to tell what is wrong with them. Avoid using the italicized words:

"Things fall because of *gravity*." (Do you see why this is not a good answer? All someone has to do is to say, "Oh, yeah!" followed by, "But what is gravity?")

"My head is round because it isn't *square*." (Why is this not such a good answer?)

"The clouds are white because they carry *water* and are *fluffy*." (Why isn't this answer good?)

House Specialty One

Perception versus Reality

To the Teacher

Objective

Students will learn to question the reliability of their observations.

Equipment

a set of binoculars or a small telescope for each group (This equipment is optional, and the experiment may be performed without it.)

8 ½-by-11-inch or larger sheets of paper

pencils

rulers

tape or staples

clipboard or equivalent

Procedure

Step 1:

Divide your class into groups of four or five students each. Have the groups select new group physicists.

Step 2:

Make simple line drawings of two to three distinct pairs of shapes on an 8 ½-by-11-inch sheet of paper, making sure that no one from the class sees the drawings. It is a good idea to use similar pairs of shapes, such as a solid and a dotted circle. You may also use different colors for the pairs.

Step 3:

Attach the sheet of drawings to a tree visible from a window or to a wall at a distance sufficient to ensure the images are not discernible with the naked eye.

Step 4:

Have students in turn observe the drawings with the naked eye and record their observations in their laboratory books. They must record that they were viewing the drawings with the naked eye, and they should estimate the distance between them and the drawings. They should not discuss their observations with their classmates—yet!

Step 5:

Have students view the drawings through the binoculars or telescope. Again, have them record their results. They must record what equipment they used (the binoculars or the telescope) and their estimated distance from the drawings. They still should not discuss their observations with their classmates.

Step 6:

After all students have completed the observations of all the drawings, have them gather again in small groups. (Do not show the original drawings to anyone yet.) Have the group physicists conduct a discussion concerning the group's observations. Do the members agree about what they observed? Have them consider the following questions:

> *How did the instruments (the binoculars, telescope, naked eye) seem to affect what they observed?*
>
> *How was distance a factor?*
>
> *In what ways are the drawings similar or dissimilar?*
>
> *Have the group physicists collect drawings from each student and present their group's observations to the whole class.*
>
> *It is a good idea to lead the discussion and to direct this activity by asking some key questions, such as why students think some or all of the diagrams are different or similar, and so on.*

Step 7:

Show the original drawings to the class and let the students observe and compare. Have an open class discussion about the students' initial *perceptions* of the drawings versus the drawings' *actual* shapes.

2 ◆ House Specialty One

To the Student

Remember to follow the laboratory book format we talked about in the introduction.

Your teacher has placed some drawings far enough away that you cannot quite make out exactly what they are just using your eyes, unless, of course, you have eagle eyes.

Step 1:

View the drawings with your naked eye and follow your teacher's directions: draw the shapes as you see them and estimate the distance you think you are from the drawings.

Step 2:

Use the binoculars or telescopes to view the diagrams again. Remember to follow your teacher's instructions and to record your observations in your laboratory book. Be sure to make a sketch of what you see, even if the drawings just look like blobs (yechh!) of ink, and to use your imagination to draw exactly what you see no matter what you think it is! Keep your results secret from everyone else (just temporarily; we are going to compare results a bit later).

Step 3:

After all members of your group have observed both drawings, gather together and follow your teacher's instructions. The group physicist leads a group discussion about your observations. Compare your drawings with those of other group members. Remember not to discuss your results with any other group member or classmate from another group. The group physicist is going to present your group's findings to the entire class as directed by your teacher, so be careful to help make a good presentation.

Step 4:

Your teacher shows the original drawings to the entire class. Compare the original drawings with what you each drew. Record the original drawings in your laboratory book.

Questions

1. Describe any differences you see between your two drawings, the first produced after observing with the naked eye and the second after observing with the binoculars or telescope. If you note any differences, why are they there? If you see no differences, why aren't there any?

2. Which figures or shapes did your group draw correctly and why? Which figures did they draw incorrectly and why?

3. On which shapes, sizes, colors, and styles of all of the shapes did your group agree? Why?

4. Did all of the diagrams change when you used the binoculars or telescope (or when you moved closer to the drawings)? What might these changes say about your *perception* of the drawings with or without the binoculars or telescope?

5. How did your drawings compare with the actual drawings of the shapes? In what ways did the instruments help? In what ways didn't they help? What differences still existed between your drawings and the originals when you used the binoculars or telescope?

6. What do you think *perception versus reality* means? Did the class discussion help answer this? If so, write down some of the responses from the class discussion in your laboratory book.

Career Note

As you will see toward the end of the book, in the tiny, tiny, tiny world of atoms are even smaller particles called electrons and protons, and we can't be sure what is happening with these minuscule particles. Such small objects behave very strangely, not in the way we think they should. Of course, we really *do not* have instruments powerful enough to allow us to see what is actually happening in objects so small; we can only rely on models or our ideas about what is happening. In the case of the imperceptible, our conceptions may be very different from reality. Are you curious? Well, you will be back . . . to study more science and physics, right?

House Specialty Two

Length and Measurement

To the Teacher

Objective

Students will understand that the distance between any two points depends on how the space in between is *traversed*, which may be in a straight or a curved line.

Equipment

ruler

string

Procedure

No group physicist is necessary; have the students work individually.

Step 1:

Select three objects easily measurable with a ruler, such as the top of a table or desk, a book, or a straight stick.

Step 2:

Select three unusually or strangely shaped objects, such as a piece of fruit (a banana, an apple, and so on), a small toy, or a crooked stick. (The word *circumference* is used in this activity, so a preliminary discussion about the word may be necessary depending on the class level.)

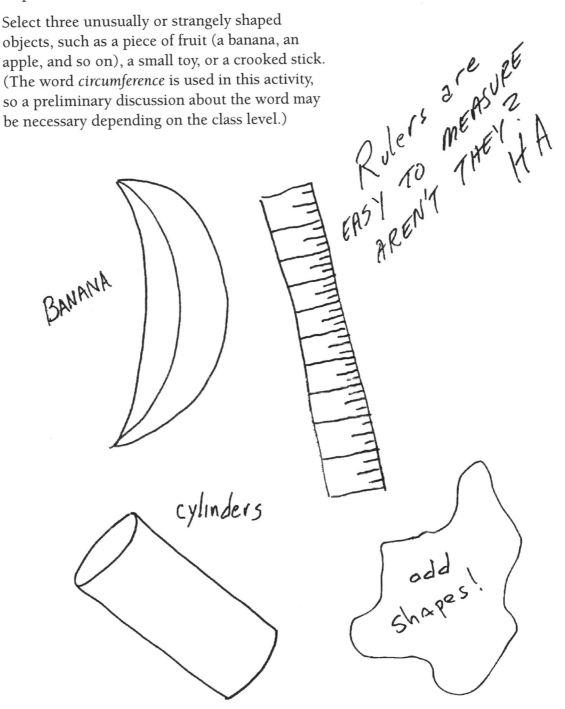

BANANA

Rulers are EASY TO MEASURE AREN'T THEY? HA

cylinders

odd shapes!

Step 3:

Guide students through the procedure.

3 ◆ House Specialty Two

To the Student

Step 1:

With your ruler in hand, measure the lengths of the objects your teacher suggests or gives to you, such as the top of a table or your desk, a book, or a long, straight stick. Do not forget to record all of your results in your laboratory book (although this activity may seem simple, it is important, you know, so no laughing, okay?).

Step 2:

Measure the circumference of the odd-shaped objects your teacher has selected. Use any equipment, such as string or a ruler, with which your teacher has supplied you. (If the word *circumference* seems a little weird, don't worry; we are going to talk all about it in the next section. For now, think of the circumference as the total outside length of an object—for instance, the circumference of a rubber ball is how long it is around.)

Questions

1. Compare the measurements you took with those your classmates took. Explain in what ways these measurements agree or disagree.

2. Since everyone had a ruler and measured the same objects, why do you think the results agree or do not agree? Give some reasons.

3. Can you think of a better way to take these measurements? Explain.

Career Note

We live in a world of four dimensions, three of space (length, width, and height) and one of time. Did you know that certain kinds of math deal with five, or fifty, or five million dimensions? (Just imagine trying to clean a bedroom with 5,000,000 dimensions. Noooo way!) This strange but beautiful type of mathematics is called *linear algebra* and is used for lots and lots of different things in science and physics. (Well, don't worry about it now, although someday you may need to know it.)

4. How did you decide which side was the length of the object? How do you know you didn't measure the width instead?

5. Look up the word *dimension* in the dictionary. Is length a dimension? Is width? How about height? Finally, is time a length or a dimension? Can you define time? (We will discuss it in more detail later, so stay tuned. And alert!)

6. How did you measure the circumference of the odd-shaped objects?

7. Are there other ways to measure these objects? Explain.

8. Did everyone agree on the measurements of these objects? Why or why not?

9. How would you measure the volume of a ball (that is, how much space it takes up)? Or better yet, a banana?

Whew! Enough questions for now, let's move on to bigger and better stuff.

Footnote 2

Look up in a dictionary the words *length*, *dimension*, and *distance*, and record the definitions in your laboratory book. Then look up the word *time* and write its definition in your book.

Footnote 3

Look in an encyclopedia or in a computer database to find out in what country and in what year the first clock was made. (This information may take some time to find, so don't give up). Who invented it?

If you are able to, find a picture of the first clock and draw or sketch it in your laboratory book. If you're lucky enough to find it on your computer database or the Internet, you might want to download a picture, print it out, and show it to the class.

Footnote 4

Find the names of some famous composers who lived about the same time as the clock was invented (not necessarily in the same country) and write a brief paragraph about each. What musical pieces did they compose?

Listen to at least one of these musical pieces. If none is available, ask your teacher to get it for you so that the whole class may hear it. (Sorry, teacher, but you have to research, too.)

House Specialty Three

A Piece of the Pi

To the Teacher

Objectives

Students will understand some of the concepts related to a circle such as its *radius* and its *diameter*.

Students will obtain the value of the constant *pi*.

Students will describe the concept of length and its measurement.

Students will use the concept of length to establish the *Pythagorean theorem* for the right triangle.

Equipment

Each group should have

a number of round cylindrical objects such as soup cans and cardboard tubes

string

rulers long enough to measure the diameters and circumferences of the cylinders and other objects

Procedure

Step 1:

Divide students into groups and have them select new group physicists.

Step 2:

Give each group the items from the equipment list.

Step 3:

Guide the students in the procedure.

Note

Perhaps the most interesting aspect of the objectives is that students will develop an appreciation for the historical dilemmas the ancient Greeks faced in their attempts to understand the circle. This section will lay much of the groundwork for future chapters.

4 ◆ House Specialty Three

To the Student

In this section you will learn some concepts regarding length as it applies to the circle. We will even explore a "new" measure, the measure of an angle as it relates to a circle. We will also explore some simple concepts such as the diameter and circumference of a circle. (Uh-oh. Remember we promised to return to this idea? Well, here we are.)

Perhaps the most important idea we will introduce will be the *constant* π (pronounced "pie," but written *pi*). Remember, *you* cannot eat this kind of pi, but your *brain* can. Since some of these ideas are a little advanced, we will just have to make them easy to understand.

This experiment is unique because we will tackle (without hurting anybody, of course) some interesting properties of the circle in the same manner that the Greeks did more than two thousand years ago.

Step 1:

Take a length of string and wrap it around one of the cylinders as shown in the following sketch.

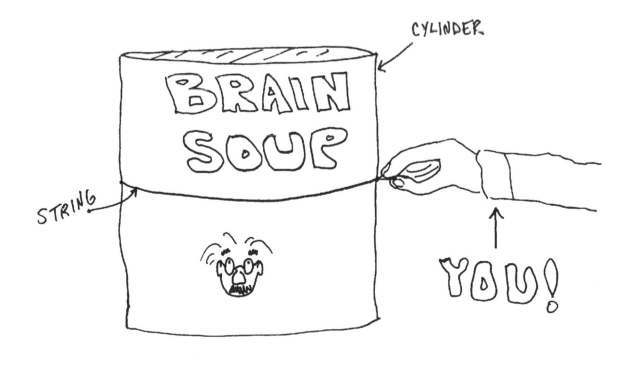

Footnote 5

Look up (research) in an encyclopedia or on your computer some early Greek philosophers and mathematicians who studied the circle. What did they say about the circle? Why were they so interested in the circle?

Step 2:

Mark on the string or cut the string where it meets. Unwrap the string.

Step 3:

Measure the length of string or the distance from the end to the mark on the string.

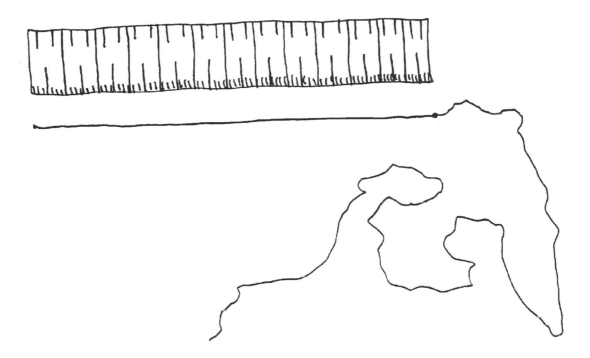

The length of the string you have just measured is the *circumference* of the cylinder. (Remember that word you defined way back when? You might say you were younger then; at least your brain was.) Every circle has a circumference.

Step 4:

Record this measurement in your laboratory book using the following format:

Circumference = _____

Okay, that's the first step, now for the second. . .

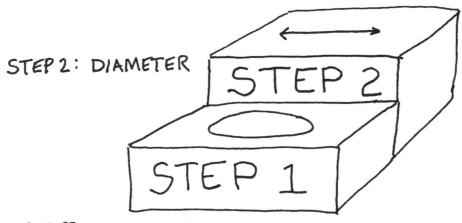

STEP 2: DIAMETER

STEP 1: CIRCUMFERENCE

Step 5:

Take your ruler and measure across the top of the tube as shown in the picture.

Be sure to place the ruler across the center of the top of the cylinder.

This distance is called the *diameter* of the cylinder (or tube).

Step 6:

Record this distance or length in your laboratory book using the following format:

Diameter = _____

Be sure to record the two measurements, circumference and diameter, very neatly in your laboratory book.

Time for the third step . . .

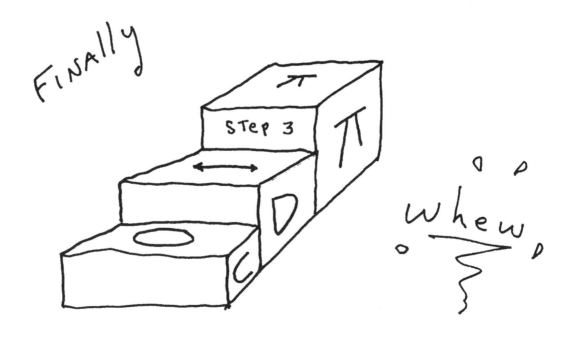

Step 7:

Divide the circumference by the diameter:

Circumference/Diameter = _____

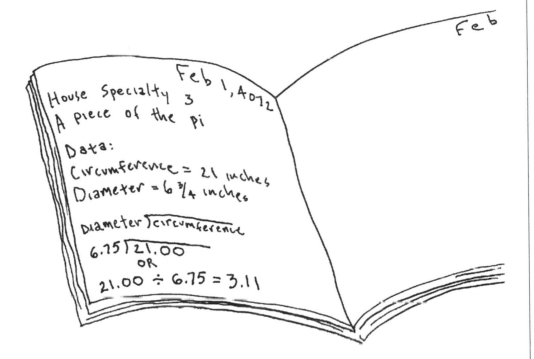

You should obtain a number slightly greater than 3. Record this number in your laboratory book.

This number is called *pi* (pronounced "pie") and is denoted by the symbol π. There is nothing mysterious about this symbol; it just stands for the number 3.1428 . . . (close to the number you obtained in this activity, right?).

> ### Note
> If you have not had decimal notation in arithmetic or if the numbers are too large for you, you may skip the next part. (Aren't you lucky.)

Pi is also called an *irrational number,* which means that the decimal part of the number (3.<u>1428</u>) continues on and on forever, and never, ever repeats a pattern.

Divide 3120 by 999. You'll find that 3120 divided by 999 = 3.<u>123123123.</u> (Note the repeating *123* after the decimal point.) Numbers that have a repeating pattern following the decimal point are called *rational* numbers; thus 3120/999 is a rational number.

You have probably noticed that your classmates and neighbors in the other groups have also calculated (or experimentally determined, as we sometimes say) the same number or one very close to the one you obtained. Note that the other groups may have even used different sized objects. Because this number turns out to be the same for all circles and cylinders, no matter what their size, we call this number a *constant.*

Footnote 6

Can you display the value of π on your calculator? You might want to compare the way your calculator displays this value with the ways in which other calculators display it. (If you don't have a calculator, ask your teacher; maybe she or he can get one to show you.)

Footnote 7

Look up in an encyclopedia the Greek alphabet and write down the first five letters.

By now you realize that the circumference of a circle divided by its diameter always equals the same number.

Wow! Gosh and more gosh! How can that be? Well, the ancient Greeks did experiments just like the one you did here, and guess what? They came up with this same strange number 3.1428 . . . (or close to it, anyway), over and over again. That is, whenever they measured the circumference and divided it by the diameter, they obtained the same (approximate) value (or quotient). Truly amazing!

They thought and thought and thought about this number and decided to try to find a way to measure it more formally. In other words, was there a way someone could measure diameters and circumferences without having to use strings and cylinders? Well, before we continue, let's consider some questions.

Questions

1. Did all the groups derive the exact same number for pi? If not, why not?

2. What other ways could you obtain this number without using any strings or tubes? (Hint: Think about using a flat sheet of paper and forming a cylinder out of the sheet. What measurements would you take?)

3. In this experiment you were told to place your ruler across the middle of the cylinder, not off to the side. Why?

4. How would you improve this experiment?

A Side Order

To the Teacher

Omit this section if it is not suitable for your students; it is not necessary for doing the remainder of the activities.

Objective

Students will approximate the value of π by using Archimedes' method of drawing polygons inside a circle.

Students will understand the mathematical difficulties in obtaining the value of π.

Equipment

ruler

paper

a drawing compass or a circular object to trace

Procedure

Have the students work individually during this experiment; groups will not be necessary. This activity is simple and elegant. Guide students through the procedure.

5 ◆ A Side Order

To the Student

Let us return to the question about finding measurements without the use of tubes and string. (Uh-oh; here it comes.)

Footnote 8

You might have stumbled across the name Archimedes when you were asked to explore the Greek philosophers in footnote 5. If you didn't, look up *Archimedes* in an encyclopedia or on a computer. In your laboratory book, write a few paragraphs about his life and what he did, answering the following questions:

- In what year was he born?

- When did he die?

- What did he invent?

We are all familiar with simple geometry, that is, with shapes that involve only straight lines, such as triangles, squares, and polygons. We also know how to find the perimeter or circumference of these objects by measuring their total outside length, right? Let's turn our attention to a slightly more complex geometry: finding the circumference of curved objects such as circles and arcs without using strings or cylinders. You might be interested in knowing that this problem baffled the greatest thinkers for thousands of years (truly amazing, isn't it?).

Well, Archimedes was one of these thinkers, and he discovered another method for measuring the perimeter (or circumference) of a circle. His method was to draw polygons, which are simply closed, straight-lined figures such as squares and rectangles, inside circles. Let's see how he did this.

Step 1:

Using your compass, draw a very large circle on your paper. Measure the diameter of this circle with you ruler, and record this number in your laboratory book using the following format:

The Diameter of the Circle = _____

(You may have to go back and review House Specialty 3 if you have forgotten the definition of *diameter*.)

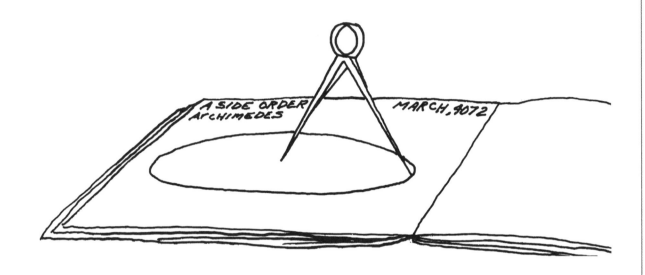

Okay,
so far
so good.

Step 2:

Divide the circle into four *equal* parts by drawing two lines through the center of the circle with your ruler, as shown. (Note that the compass point marks the center of the circle, right?)

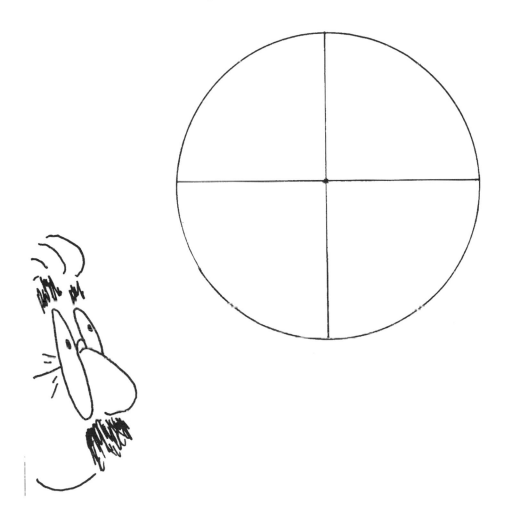

If you did this just right, these two lines should be at right angles (90 degrees) to each other. These two lines are said to be *perpendicular* to each other. We can pretend this is a birthday cake and we want to divide the cake into equal parts. Since your cake is already divided into four equal parts, we will draw two more lines that will divide it into eight equal parts.

Step 3:

Draw the lines as best you can using a ruler or other straight edge and refer to the diagram that follows, noting how the ends (or tips) of the lines intersecting the circle are numbered in the pictures.

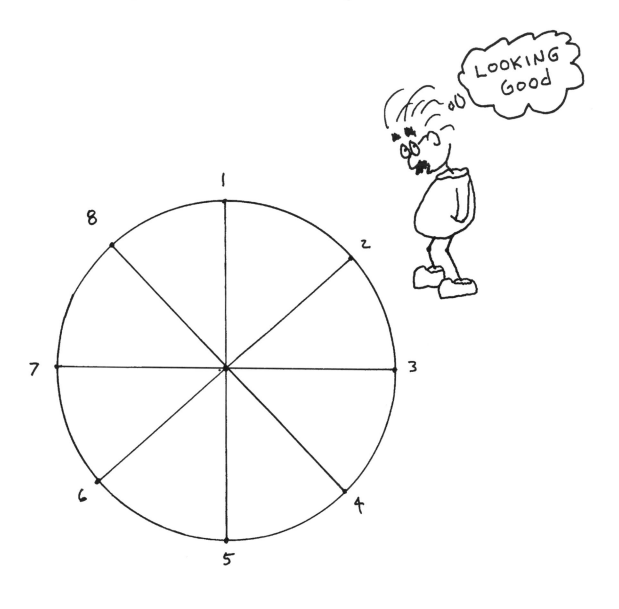

Step 4:

Connect the intersection points numbered 2, 4, 6, and 8 with straight lines as shown in the following diagram. You should have a square shape drawn inside the circle. Do you?

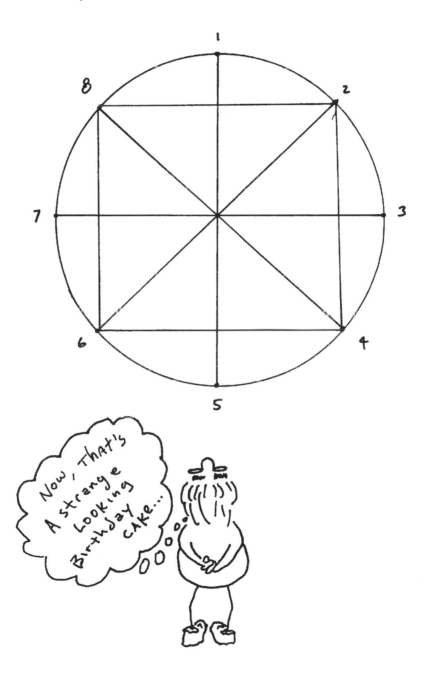

Getting tired? Do not give up yet and don't worry (we keep saying that, huh?); things are just beginning to get interesting. Let's summarize what we have done so far.

We have just drawn the largest and only true square that will fit inside your circle.

Well, here it comes again; you might as well start thinking about this last step because (you guessed it) more questions are coming.

Step 5:

Measure the length of each side of this square with a ruler, and add these lengths together. (If it is a perfect square, we should only have to measure the length of one side and multiply by 4, right?) This total length of the square is called the *perimeter* of the square. (You may also call this the circumference of your square. Do you see why?)

Step 6:

Record this value in your laboratory book using the following format:

The Perimeter (or circumference) of the square = _____

Step 7:

Divide the perimeter (or circumference) of this square by the diameter of the circle to obtain the following, and record it in your laboratory book using the following format:

Perimeter of the square ÷ the diameter of the circle = _____

This value is the first measured value using the square polygon.

Label it as follows in your laboratory book:

First value of π using the square in the circle =

_____

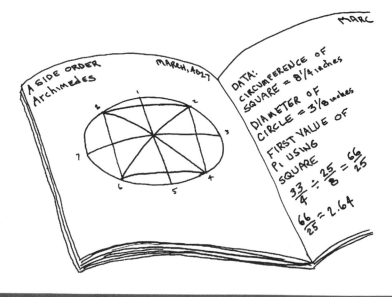

Now hold on. Try to follow this next step closely; we're going to do it again.

Step 8.

Let's repeat the whole process, this time using an eight-sided figure, or octagon, drawn inside the circle to calculate a second value of π. Follow the diagram closely and observe that the octagon is formed by connecting all eight points on the circle, thus forming the eight-sided figure:

Step 9:

Guess what you have to do now? That's right! Measure the perimeter (or circumference) of the octagon this time, and divide this number by the diameter of the circle. This value becomes your second value of π:

The Perimeter (or circumference) of the octagon =_____

Perimeter of the octagon ÷ the diameter of the circle = _____

Step 10:

Label this as your second value of π in your laboratory book:

Second value of π using the octagon in the circle = _____

Did you notice that the octagon looks more like the circle than does the square? Of course you did!

Following are a few more questions to make you crazy.

What do you think would happen if you drew a ten- or twelve-sided shape inside the circle? Do you suppose that these shapes (actually, we call them *polygons*) would look more and more like the circle? Well, draw these shapes inside the circle and find out!

You are probably seeing now what Archimedes had in mind and what he was trying to do, right? Well, if not, let's see if we can guess. It seems as though he was using straight-lined shapes that approached the curved shape of a circle because the total perimeter (or circumference) of straight-lined shapes, such as the square and the octagon, can easily be measured using a ruler or other straight edge. Note, too, that the more sides a figure has, the more the figure begins to look like a circle.

Summarize the results in your laboratory book by recording the following, using the following format:

The first value of pi using the square = _____

The second value of pi using the octagon = _____

This method of measuring is the *Archimedean method.*

Restaurant at the Beginning of the Universe © 1997 Zephyr Press, Tucson, Arizona

Questions

1. Which of your values is closer to the true value of π? Why?

2. What would happen if you were to continue drawing polygons with more and more sides inside the circle and dividing the perimeters by the diameter of the circle? Would your values for π become more accurate? Why?

3. What problems with this method do you see?

4. Here it comes—we warned you . . . We told you earlier that when you draw a square in a circle using the preceding method, the square is the largest and only true square that can be drawn inside the circle. Is this statement true? Did your square appear to be a square or more like a rectangle? Or worse, a lopsided rectangle?

5. If you traced the shape of a can or cylinder to draw your circle, how did you find the center of the circle?

6. When you drew the octagon, you divided the circle into eight equal sections. Describe the method you used to do this. Can you think of a way to ensure that the sections are equal? Describe the way. After all, if you just "eyeballed" your lines then you probably ended up with a "wobbly," disoriented-looking square or octagon, right?

7. If your sections were exactly equal, then you should have had a very healthy looking square and octagon. Can you think of better ways to create equal sections rather than using your eye?

A Quick Peek at the Buffet

Right or Wrong Triangles

To the Teacher

Objectives

Students will identify relationships between the angles and the sides of triangles.

Students will observe the results of the Pythagorean theorem.

Equipment

paper

graph paper

scissors

rulers

Procedure

Step 1:

Divide the class into new groups, as usual, having them select new group physicists.

Step 2:

Inform the groups that the group physicists will present the results to the class at the end of the activity.

Step 3:

Have each student obtain a collection of the equipment for the activity, and guide the students through the experiment.

6 ◆ A Quick Peek at the Buffet

To the Student

This House Specialty is some of the best brain food around. We are talking about a healthy serving of triangles smothered in hot, steamy angles, with generous servings of lengths and sides, of course topped off with the delicious Pythagorean theorem (yum, yum).

Okay, here we go.

Step 1:

The first thing to do is draw a triangle on your plain sheet of paper. Any kind of triangle will do; just be sure to use your ruler and draw nice straight lines.

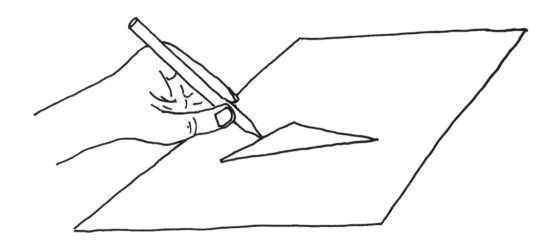

Restaurant at the Beginning of the Universe © 1997 Zephyr Press, Tucson, Arizona

Step 2:

Label the angles of your triangle by numbering them 1, 2, and 3, as shown in the following diagram. (Hey, maybe that is why we call this shape or figure a *tri-angle*.)

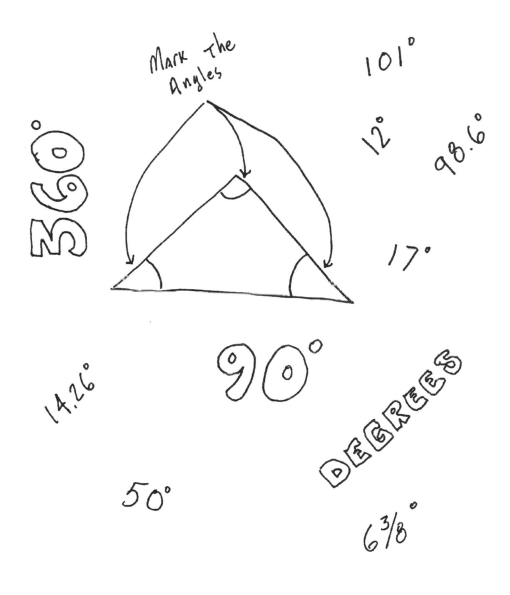

Step 3:

Being careful to note where the numbers are,

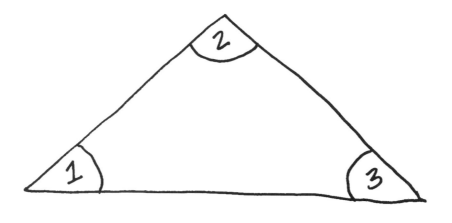

carefully cut out the triangle from
the paper with your scissors,

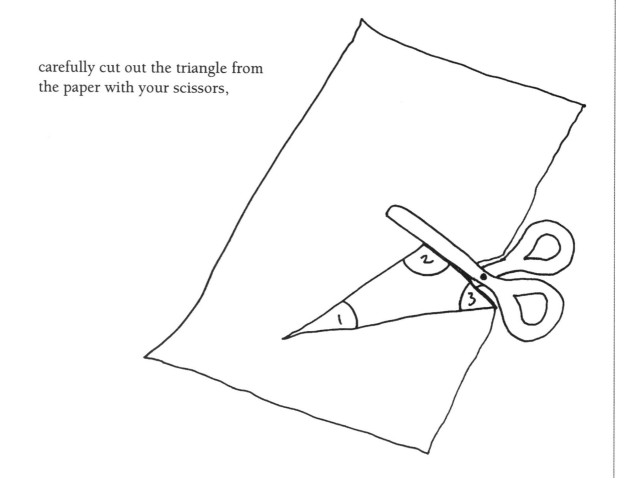

and tear—that's right, tear—off the numbered corners from your triangle to obtain three numbered angles.

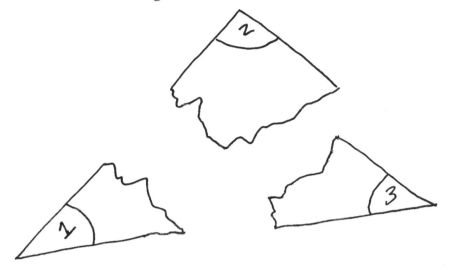

Okay, okay, you're probably wondering what all of this means. Well, there is a point to it after all, so just hold on and you will see.

Step 4:

Place the three numbered corners that you just tore off together in numbered order. That is, place angle 1 next to angle 2, then place angle 3 next to angle 2, as shown in the following sketch.

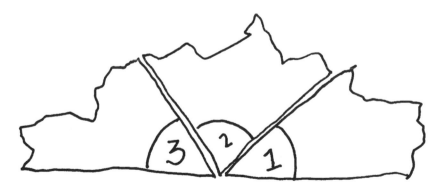

What do you see? The three angles of your triangle form a straight line. This straight line happens regardless of the shape or type of triangle you drew.

Step 5:

Try this process again using any other drawn triangle. Notice that no matter how you draw the triangle, the sum of the three angles of any triangle forms a straight line.

Note, too, that the pieces of the triangle also form a sort of half circle. Now a full circle is said to have 360 degrees. (Just some nice number we picked at random. Or did we?) Thus the sum of the angles of a triangle forming a straight line, sort of a diameter of a circle, consists of one-half a full circle, or 360/2 = 180 degrees.

Footnote 9

See if you can find out why 360 degrees was selected to be the total number of degrees in a circle. (Do you think it may have something to do with the way we tell the time?)

Let's do another activity. This time we are going to use graph paper. (If you don't have graph paper, you can make your own.) Note that the graph paper consists of equal-size squares or boxes; we are going to use these little squares in this activity so pay special attention to them, okay?

6 ◆ A Quick Peek at the Buffet *(continued)*

Step 1:

Using your ruler, draw a vertical or horizontal line three little squares in length on your graph paper. Don't place your line too close to the edge of the graph paper; there should be plenty of free squares around it.

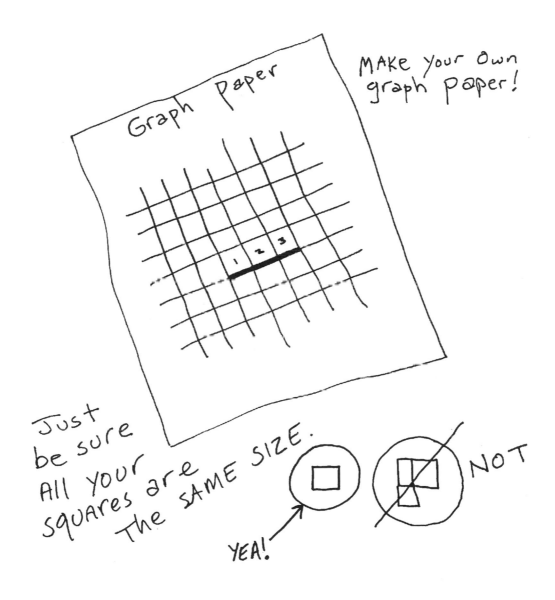

Step 2:

Okay. At one end of this first line draw a second line four squares long and perpendicular (remember what that means?) to the first line. Whew! Did you understand all of that? If you are not confused by now you should be. Soooo, check out the picture.

Step 3:

Connect the two free ends of both lines to make a triangle.

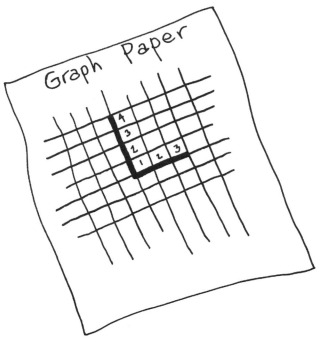

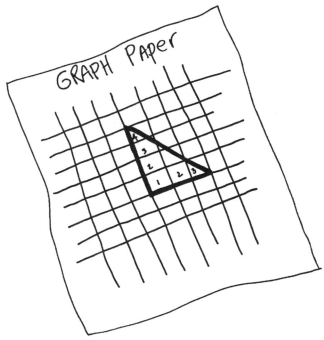

Now, you have drawn many triangles before (maybe), but let's dive a little deeper into this one. This type of triangle is called a *right triangle* because, as you have drawn it, one of its angles is 90 degrees (or one-fourth of a circle).

(One may wonder: If there is a right triangle, might there be a wrong triangle?)

Okay, okay, let's get back to it.

This next part is rather tricky, so be careful. You may need to read it a few times to get it just right, so ask your teacher to help just a little bit; be patient and have fun.

Notice now that you have a right triangle with one side that is four little squares long and another side that is three little squares long; the sides of a triangle are called its *legs*.

Step 4:

Using the 4-square-long leg, draw a complete square box off of this leg 4 units by 4 units, and note that the total number of little squares (count them) within this boxed area on the graph paper is 16, or 4 times 4.

Step 5:

Do the same for the 3-square-long leg. This square consists of 9 (or 3 times 3) little squares on the graph paper.

Okay. Now what we have is a right triangle with a square on one leg and another square on the other leg. Notice that the total number of little squares on both legs is 25, that is, 16 little squares on one leg + 9 little squares on the other leg = 25 little squares.

Why do all this? Hold on; here we go . . .

Step 6:

Take another sheet of graph paper and place it along the side of the triangle that doesn't have a square on it. (By the way, this side is called the *hypotenuse*—funny word, right?) Count the number of squares that make up the length of this third leg as illustrated. This number should be exactly 5, or close to it.

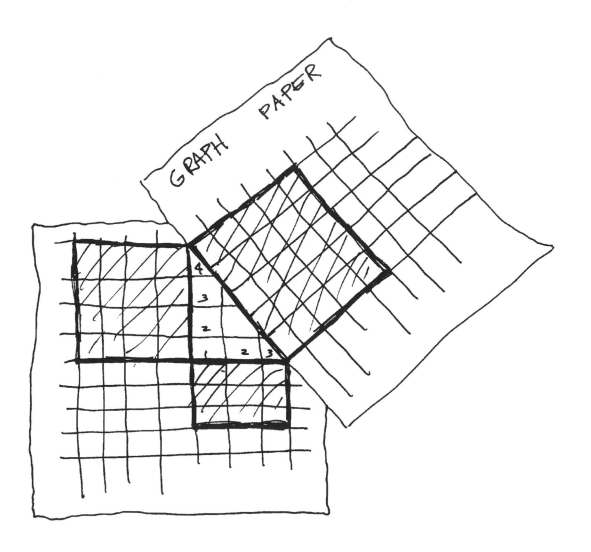

Step 7:

Do the same thing we did before; draw a square on this third side and count the total number of squares in it, which should be 25, or 5 times 5, little squares.

Notice that we now have three boxes, two boxes on the legs that we first drew and the new box we just drew on the third leg.

Now, let's see what we have. Well, it appears as though the total number of little squares making up the box on the third leg, 25, is the same as the total number of little squares on the two boxes on the other legs, 16 + 9. We may restate this fact: the sum of all the little squares on the two sides of a right triangle is equal to the total number of little squares on the third side. This is called the *Pythagorean theorem*.

Footnote 10

Try the preceding activity, but use a triangle that is not a right triangle. See if the theorem works in this case.

Footnote 11

Look up the Greek philosopher and mathematician Pythagoras. Write a brief biography about him. Be sure you answer the following questions.

- ■ When was he born?
- ■ Where was he born?
- ■ What did he do in his life?

Look up *Pythagorean theorem* in an encyclopedia and write a description of it in your laboratory book.

A Sweet Treat

Mass

To the Teacher

Objective

Students will distinguish between mass and weight.

Equipment

pens

pencils

eraser

books

paper

coins

Procedure

Step 1:

Divide the class into the usual groups and have them choose new group physicists.

Step 2:

Have students each select the following objects from the classroom or their toolbox—a pen, a pencil, an eraser, a book, a piece of crumpled paper, and a penny.

Step 3:

Students individually separate their collections into two categories: objects they think are heavy and those they think are light.

Step 4:

Have students write in their laboratory books brief descriptions of each object in the two categories. Encourage students to use words such as *shape, color, size, mass,* and *weight.*

Step 5:

Have the group physicists lead a discussion about the results. Have them first list the objects each person considered heavy and those each considered light. Does everyone agree? Are there objects about which the whole group agree (that is, everyone in one group categorized the pen and the eraser as heavy)? Are there some objects about which there was no agreement (that is, some group members categorized the penny as light, some, heavy)?

Step 6:

Have the group physicist lead the group to agree on which objects are heavy and which are light.

Step 7:

Have the group describe the objects in each category, using the descriptions they recorded individually. (The purpose is for students to exhibit that the concepts of heavy and light are subjective, that is, subject to relational interpretation.) Lead the class into a discussion about its findings, and note that some groups may agree that heavy and round is a more important description than heavy and blue. Also discuss these types of connections and why these connections may lead to some misconceptions and misinterpretations, that is, a small eraser may be much heavier than a large pen, so small and light are not necessarily connected traits.

7 ◆ A Sweet Treat

To the Student

In one of your earlier activities you learned that what we perceive or observe may be quite different from what really exists. (Remember the binoculars and the drawings?) Well, as an ambassador of science, you should begin to observe everything around you and your world. You should be asking lots of questions about what you see, and you should try to answer some of these questions on your own. For instance, we use the word *mass* or a derivative quite often, don't we? "Hey, look at that mountain; it's gigantic and has a mass." "Say, that jet plane sure looks massive." But what exactly is mass? Is the mass of an object the same as its weight (that is, does *mass* mean the same thing as *weight?*) When you weigh yourself on a scale, what are you measuring? Does an object's mass have any relation to any of its other measurements, such as its length, height, or width? How is it that a massive battleship floats in water, whereas a small rock or pebble simply sinks? These questions are very interesting, but more important, some of these questions actually have answers. However, remember that these questions took many hundreds, sometimes even thousands, of years to answer. The answers to many of these questions actually lead to other questions, and that is where you come in; we are going to answer many questions and see what questions they lead to.

Step 1:

Collect six different objects from the classroom or from your laboratory toolbox, such as a pen, a pencil, an eraser, a book, a piece of crumpled paper, and a penny. Remember to follow your teacher's instructions carefully.

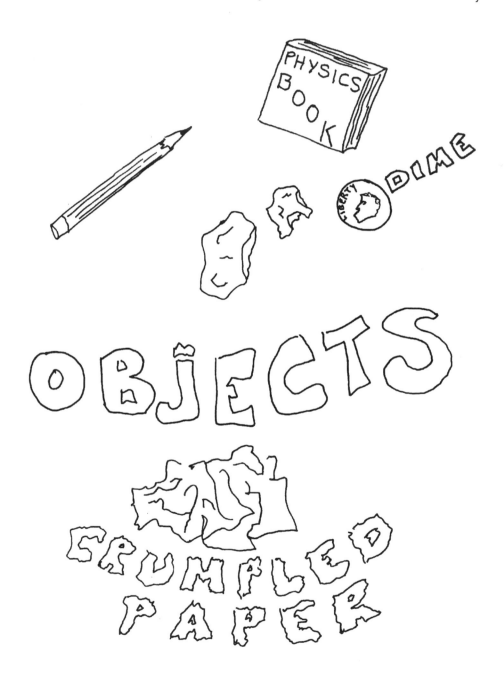

Step 2:

Divide your group of six objects into two categories: in the first category, place those objects you consider to be heavy; in the second, those objects you consider to be light. (You don't have to divide them evenly, such as three heavy and three light; any combination is okay. Just use your best judgment, and remember there is no right or wrong way to do this.)

Step 3:

Now follow your teacher's instructions to describe each of these objects in their respective categories; that is, describe as many features as you can about the heavy objects and as many features as you can about the light objects. Use your imagination and consider such things as shape, color, size, and weight.

Step 4:

Record all of your observations and conclusions in your laboratory book.

Step 5:

Your group physicist will lead your group in a discussion about your results and observations. Your group discussion should focus on the following ideas:

Is there one quality that best describes each object?

Is there one quality that all the objects have in common?

Are all the objects blue? Straight? Crooked? Made of wood?

Do all the objects appear to weigh the same?

Do the objects feel heavy or light in your hand?

Remember to use your imagination and to have lots of fun with this activity. Why? Because there are no right or wrong answers.

Okay, now it's time to liven things up a little bit, with another activity. The group physicists from each group will perform a simple experiment.

Okay group physicist, here we go:

Step 1:

Stand straight and tall and hold the eraser in one hand and the penny in the other. Now hold them out at the same height from the floor, and release them at the same time, letting them fall to the floor. Everyone in your group should carefully watch them fall.

(You may need to repeat this activity a few times. That's okay; the penny and eraser need the exercise. Right?)

Step 2:

Record the following data in your laboratory book:

> Describe what you observed.

> Which object fell faster?

> Explain what you observed.

Guess what? You just performed the same kind experiment that Galileo Galilei did more than four hundred years ago. Galileo dropped two rocks, one light and one heavy, from the top of the leaning tower of Pisa, in Italy. Do you know what happened in Galileo's experiment?

Footnote 12

Look up Galileo Galilei in an encyclopedia or, of course, in the library. (Let's not forget the library—it's a great place!) Write a brief biography (a paragraph or two) about Galileo in your laboratory book.

Find another famous person, such as a writer, a composer, or an artist, who lived at the same time as Galileo, and write a brief biography in your laboratory book.

Step 3:

Okay, group physicist, ask for a volunteer from your group to repeat what you just did, but this time use two different objects, such as the pencil and the book. Don't forget; be careful and release both objects from the same height at the same time.

Step 4:

Record your observations and conclusions in your laboratory book. Consider the following questions:

Did all the objects fall in the same way?

Imagine that the eraser and the penny had the same weight. Would they land at the same time? Why or why not?

Step 5:

Take any two objects from your collection and repeat this experiment. Record your observations. (Reminder: you should be recording all questions in your laboratory book—physics takes work, work, work, but it can be fun, too, you know.)

Notice that the word *mass* has not been used for any of these activities, but by now you might be suspecting that weight and mass may have something to do with all of this. Well, let's see.

Suppose you repeated the experiment using the book and the pencil. You know they fall at the same time, but which would be easier to catch when they reached the floor? Well, you probably don't have to do this experiment (in fact, you probably should not do it) to know that the book would be much harder to catch after falling a few feet, right? Well, there we have it: the book contains more mass, so we say it weighs more and it is much harder to stop or catch than the pencil. But this phenomenon doesn't help explain why all objects (heavy or light) reach the floor at the same time when released at the same time and from the same height. Galileo asked himself the same question and did have some ideas of how to explain it. It looks like you'll have to read on to see what he thought and how he figured it out.

Here's how it goes: Suppose you take three pennies and drop them at the same time. Since they are approximately the same weight, you suspect they will fall at the same rate, right? Certainly!

Now repeat the experiment, this time stacking two of the pennies together. Now you have two objects, one a single penny and the other, the two stacked pennies. Release both from rest at the same time and from the same height. They should still fall at the same rate just like before. But this time you dropped one penny with one-half the mass of the other stacked pennies, right?

Okay let's try another interesting activity.

Step 1:

As a class, select a volunteer.

Step 2:

Have the volunteer take an uncrumbled sheet of paper and release it with another object, such as the coin, pencil, or eraser, as you did before. Describe individually in your laboratory book what you observe.

Step 3:

Have the volunteer repeat the experiment one more time, this time crumbling the paper sheet before dropping it. Again record your observations.

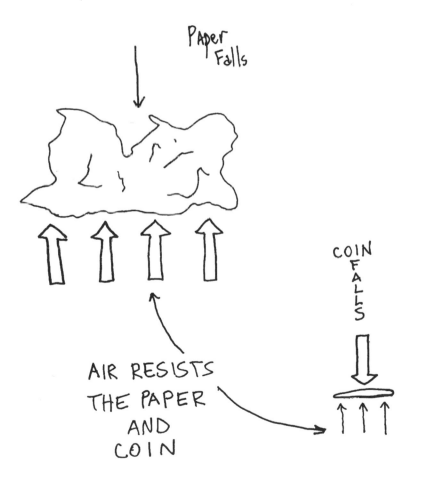

The air around us tends to resist an object's motion. The flat paper has more surface area than does the coin or eraser, so it must fight against more air as it falls; it just cannot fall as fast. When you used the crumpled paper, it fell much faster than the flat sheet and almost kept up with the other objects. (It still has a bit more surface area than the other objects, so it may fall a bit slower.)

But why does a very large rock fall at the same rate as a small rock? Since a large rock has a larger surface area, shouldn't it fall very slowly? Hmmmm, and more hmmmm.

Galileo could not answer this question. It was answered about fifty years after Galileo, by someone you have probably heard of before: Sir Isaac Newton. Sir Isaac thought and thought and thought about this question and finally discovered that all objects have a quantity called *mass*. Also, all objects fall at the same rate of speed no matter what their mass is when there is no air resistance. That is why a large rock and a small rock land at about the same time—the air resistance just isn't strong enough to slow them down much.

> ### Career Note
> You'll never believe what happens to an object's mass as its speed approaches the speed of light. Zoooom!

Now, wait a minute, something here is just a little puzzling, don't you think?

If air resistance is responsible for slowing down the motion of a falling objects, then doesn't that mean that if there were no air present (which we call a vacuum), the flat paper and the coin would land at the same time? Well, there is the answer; in other words, if there were no air to resist the motion, then a feather and a pound of iron, a jet airliner, a pillow, and even the space shuttle would fall at the same rate.

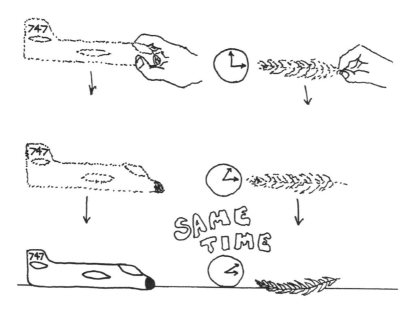

Footnote 13

Look up Sir Isaac Newton in an encyclopedia, on your computer, or in the library. Write a brief biography about him in your laboratory book.

Sir Isaac had a very good friend who used Isaac's research to discover a comet that visits Earth every seventy-two years. This comet now goes by his last name. Find the name of Sir Isaac's friend. (Hint: His first name was Edmund.)

Find a famous artist from Sir Isaac's time, and write a paragraph about him or her.

There is still something askew about mass and weight, however. How is mass different from weight? For example, you might already know that the Apollo astronauts, with their spacesuits and equipment, weighed about 330 pounds on Earth but only 55 pounds on the Moon! Since weight changes depending on whether you live on Earth or the Moon, does that mean that mass changes, too? What do you think?

Well, that's the question Sir Isaac tried to answer by believing that an object's mass would not change if it were placed on the Moon, even though its weight would. Remember what we asked before—"Which would be easier to catch after falling a few feet, a book or a pencil?"

Sir Isaac reasoned that there was a force of gravity on Earth and a force of gravity on the Moon. The force of gravity on the Moon, however, is much weaker than the force of gravity on Earth (you will learn more about this new force called *gravity* a little later on). Another way to say this is that Earth actually pulls you down with a greater force than the Moon does.

The idea here is that this force of gravity can only work or act on an object's mass. So, to sum it up, the force of gravity acts on a mass and gives you a measure of the object's weight. Thus, an object such as a pencil "weighs" more on Earth than it does on the Moon because of the difference in gravitational force.

As you continue your careers as investigators of science, you will learn enough about physics to be able to calculate your own mass.

Career Note
You will eventually learn other really great things, like how time slows down as you go super, super fast. Also, time goes slower on Jupiter than it does on Earth. Guess what? Time also has something to do with different gravitational forces.

Restaurant at the Beginning of the Universe © 1997 Zephyr Press, Tucson, Arizona

Acceleration

When we say that something is traveling at 50 miles per hour, we are referring to its *speed.* If the speed doesn't change, then the object is said to be moving at a *constant speed* or, as young physicists like to say, at a *constant velocity.*

Have you ever stepped onto a bus and lurched toward the rear as it began to move? Have you ever been pushed against the back of your seat on an airplane as it began to take off? Well, when this happens, you have experienced what is called *acceleration.* Now recall that once the bus reaches a constant speed or when the airplane reaches its cruising speed, you don't experience this lurching toward the rear of the bus or the push against the airplane seat, right? You might remember that you can move about with ease, as if you were not moving at all. This phenomenon is the basic difference between an object moving at a constant velocity and one that is accelerating.

Mathematically (don't run and hide, now!) we say,

Acceleration = the change in velocity ÷ the time it takes to change the velocity

Sometimes we abbreviate this equation:

$A = Velocity \div Time$, or

$$A = V/T$$

Home Activity

To the Teacher

Objective

Students will distinguish between the concepts of velocity and acceleration.

Equipment

any objects from the students' laboratory toolbox or the classroom

Procedure

The following activity can be performed either at home or in the classroom. However, if you choose to do the activity in class, we suggest that students take a few days to record what they observe outside the classroom as an integral part of this activity. Lead the students in the following procedure.

8 ◆ Home Activity

To the Student

Galileo was very curious about acceleration, so in order to study it more closely, he invented an ingenious technique that helped to slow down the motion of the objects he was studying. If he could see how these objects moved, he reasoned, he might be able to attain a greater understanding of how the universe made objects do the things they do as they move through space. You might think of this as watching a movie or a video in "slow motion," a technique that allows you to see with ease all the details you might have missed at the normal speed.

Now let's look at what he did. You already know that when you throw a ball into the air, it starts off fast, comes to a halt, then returns, right?

No velocity

SO FAR SO GOOD

YIPES!

starts off fast

then, because of gravity, it begins to slow down or decelerate, then stops at greatest height;

then it returns to Earth.

If its velocity were constant, then the ball would start off with some velocity

and never return . . .

Well, Galileo would throw things up into the air and notice they were accelerating. The problem was that the action was too fast for him to measure (there were no digital stopwatches back then. No MTV, either . . . poor guy!). His problem was how to slow the motion of an object thrown or projected upward in the air so he could measure the speed.

Well, to solve this problem, instead of throwing the object into the air he simply took a long board and tilted it slightly, like so . . .

Physicists and scientists call this an *inclined plane*.

Then he put the object, maybe a ball (since it can roll freely), at the top of the incline . . .

and watched it roll down the inclined plane. He immediately noticed that the ball was always picking up speed, going faster and faster and faster as it traveled down the incline.

He decided to adjust the angle of the inclined plane to make it steeper, which made the ball increase its velocity until it was going even faster than before. Finally, when the plane was vertical, the ball just fell as if dropped.

8 ◆ Home Activity (continued)

What do Galileo's observations mean? Well, remember what we said before: When objects and masses accelerate, such as the ball in Galileo's experiment, they gain or lose some speed as time passes, and we say the ball experiences an acceleration, right?

For example, if the ball were traveling at 1 mile per hour at the end of the first second, it might gain speed until, at the end of the next second, it is traveling at 3 miles per hour, then maybe at 8 miles per hour at the end of the third second, and so on. In contrast, if the object is moving at a constant velocity, then the object would start at some value, say 2 miles per hour, and would simply remain at that value at the end of every second, forever (kind of boring, right?).

In order to calculate the acceleration of the ball on the inclined plane, Galileo used his heartbeat as a clock to measure time. Why wouldn't that work very well?

You are to do this activity at home. You may require a few days to complete it.

Step 1:

Repeat Galileo's experiment with the inclined planes. You can use a very long board propped up at one end as an incline.

Step 2:

Find a few objects that can roll down your incline, say, various sizes of marbles, maybe a can of soup, or even a penny or a nickel placed on edge.

(Things that you should not use are small animals: cats, dogs, or fish.)

Step 3:

Roll the objects down the incline, then drop a few of them. Compare the way the objects roll down the incline (accelerate) to the way objects that are simply dropped fall. Notice that the incline slows the acceleration of the object just a little bit and you can observe its motion changing; that is, you may observe its speed increasing as it moves down the incline.

Step 4:

Answer the following questions in your laboratory book.

Will you need a long incline plane or a short incline plane to observe this "slowing down" of the acceleration?

Does the angle (or height of the incline elevation) affect the acceleration?

Do different sized objects appear to accelerate differently for the same incline elevation? (That is, which appears to be slowed down more, a small marble or a large one?)

Step 5:

For the next few days, find several objects that travel at a constant velocity. List them in your laboratory book for a class discussion. Also find several objects that accelerate or don't move at a constant velocity. List these in your laboratory book, again for a classroom discussion.

As you look around your universe, what do observe more of: objects that accelerate or objects that travel at constant velocity? Don't forget to look at lots of things around you, such as birds, airplanes flying overhead, dogs and cats running around, and so on . . . have fun!

Follow your teacher's instructions to participate in a classroom discussion following your observations.

9

House Specialty Four

Force

Now that you are familiar with mass and acceleration, two very important concepts in physics, you're going to discover that guess what—they are related (just like cousins). (Seems like everything in the world of physics has a relative, doesn't it?)

Well, okay, now that we've said this, you're probably not surprised that we are going to explore this relationship in this section of our delicious menu.

Remember when your brain feasted on the House Specialty way back when the concept of *area* was introduced? Back then you learned that when you multiplied the length of a rectangle (or square) times its width you obtained its area. You may have to review that House Specialty again if you have forgotten it.

Now let's imagine that we have a rectangle like the one shown, except in place of the width as a measurement, we are going to insert mass (that is, the width represents the amount of mass that an object contains). You might say that if 2 inches represents 4 kilograms (a *kilogram* is just a unit or name we use for a mass), then 4 inches represents how much mass? This discussion simply means that the size of the mass is determined by the width of our rectangle.

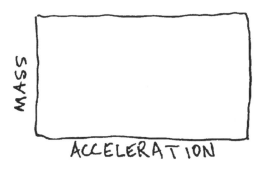

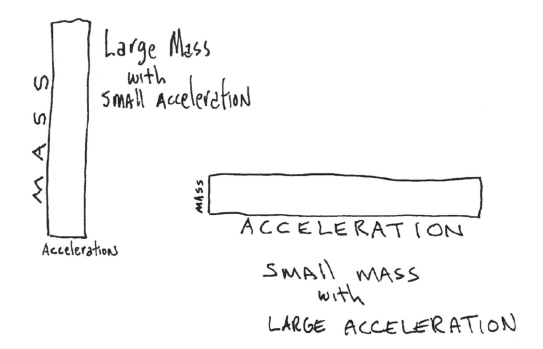

We represent the acceleration of an object in the same way; that is, the length of our rectangle represents the amount of its acceleration. Do you see how this representation works? The following is an example: The mass of a jumbo jet is very large; the mass of a flea will be very tiny. In the case of a jumbo jet taking off, we know it is accelerating very quickly, so its mass and acceleration are very large. But the flea taking off has a small acceleration and a small mass.

Can you guess what the rectangle would look like if the flea or jumbo jet were standing still (no acceleration at all)? Try drawing it for yourself now. (Hint: The acceleration is zero but the mass is not.)

Well, it turns out that Sir Isaac Newton showed us that when any mass accelerates, there is a force associated with it (or, as we say, the force "causes" the acceleration). How do we calculate this force? That's easy. If we know an object's mass and its acceleration, then the force turns out to be just the area inside our mass-acceleration rectangle. We'll call this rectangle *Newton's rectangle*. The jumbo jet has a very large force, whereas the flea's is very, very tiny.

You just learned Newton's second law of motion—force is equal to mass times acceleration. That is, the area of Newton's rectangle represents the force that is acting on the mass. See how easy that is?

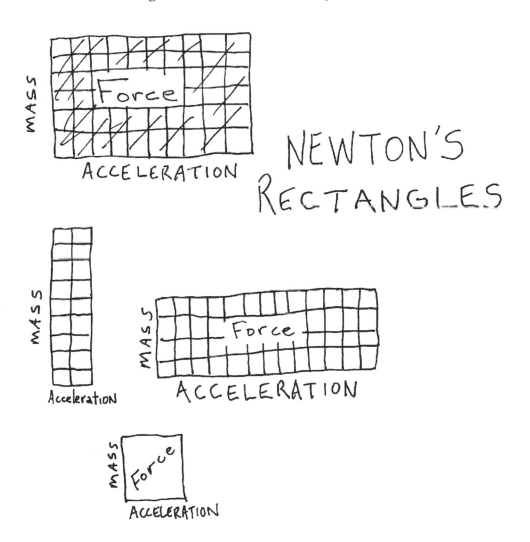

Now, if there is a second law, do you suppose there is a first law, or a third law?

Footnote 14

Look up Newton's laws of motion in the encyclopedia, on your computer, or in the library. Simply write them down in your laboratory book, even if they are hard to understand at this point. (Don't worry, we'll discuss them in time.) Just having them in your book is very important.

We still have much to discuss concerning the nature of forces and this new law. For example, what do you think the answers to the following questions are?

If a car is traveling at a constant velocity, does that mean there is not a force acting on the car?

Can an object exert a force on itself?

Do all forces exerted on masses arise from contact with other masses?

Do some objects refuse to accelerate even though forces are acting on them?

Let's consider the last question. Have you ever leaned against a wall? Well, your leaning certainly exerts a force on the wall, but does the wall accelerate? We hope not! Right? Have you tried to answer the other questions? Getting curious? Are you wondering why? Do you want to know some answers? If so, then let's move on to our Late Night Snack . . .

10

Late Night Snack

Force in the Real World

To the Teacher

Objectives

Students will apply the definition of force to specific applications.

Students will determine that air resistance is a force.

Equipment

a clear container, preferably a small aquarium or large jar that will hold water

two objects that sink in water (Two small rocks or pebbles will work just fine. They should be roughly the same size and weight.)

an object that floats (A wooden block, a cork, or both will be suitable.)

Equipment *(continued)*

a glass or beaker

some colored water (or iced tea)

a small bubble level

a 4-by-4-inch piece of aluminum foil

a large paper clip

Procedure

Have students form new groups and select new group physicists. Guide students throughout the following set of activities. Have students answer all questions and record all answers in their laboratory books.

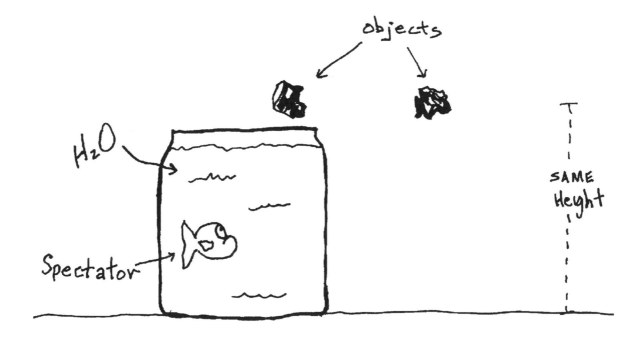

When you do the experiment, suspend the two rocks as illustrated. They should be at the same height, slightly above the surface of the water (to avoid splashing). Release both rocks at the same time.

10 ◆ Late Night Snack

To the Student

You have learned that force is related to mass and acceleration. You need to understand these concepts to relish the tasty morsels in this Late Night Snack. We think you will find this late night snack tasty indeed; furthermore, you will learn some fascinating applications of the previous House Specialty (maybe even some of the answers to the questions raised in the last section).

You know that any time a mass accelerates there must be a force lurking somewhere. Your teacher is going to do a simple experiment that you have already seen demonstrated many times before. Have you ever dropped something heavy in a swimming pool or bathtub and watched it sink? Or float? Why do some objects sink while others don't? If you answered the last question by saying, "Objects sink because they're heavy and float because they are light," then explain how an iron battleship floats. It is made of very heavy metal, you know (not the kind of heavy metal you listen to, though).

Your teacher will drop one object in the water-filled container and the other outside the container. Observe that both are the same distance above the table and that your teacher releases them at the same time.

Did the rocks hit the ground and the bottom of the container at the same time? Why or why not? Record your observations in your laboratory book.

As you saw previously (check your laboratory book), all objects fall at the same rate regardless of their mass (ignoring air resistance); however, in this experiment, the two rocks fell at different rates. You might remember that you saw something like this before. Recall a few menu items back, when you released the flat sheet of paper and an eraser or pencil, the same thing happened. (See why we need laboratory books?) We know that air resistance can affect how fast an object falls, so perhaps you're thinking that water behaves just like air: it resists an object's motion.

Given your knowledge of physics at this point, record in your laboratory book your explanation of the result of this experiment. (Hint: Force and some kind of resistance must play a role, right?)

Have you ever tried walking in a pool, the ocean, or a lake and noticed how difficult it is? If you haven't, then try doing the 100-yard dash in a wading pool sometime.

Let's think this through together. The rock released in the air certainly fell much faster than the rock released in the aquarium, right? Well, because both rocks (masses) were accelerated by the same force (gravity) but fell at different rates (accelerations), then we must conclude that the water resisted the rock's normal acceleration caused by gravity. This difference in acceleration must mean that the water exerted its own force on the rock, which opposed the force of gravity on the rock. We call this force a *resistive force.*

Now let's answer some questions. Okay, group physicists, lead a group discussion to answer the following questions:

Does air exert a resistive force on a flat piece of paper when it falls?

Does air exert a resistive force on a rock or pebble when it falls?

(Don't forget to record your answers in your book.)

Okay, let's do another experiment. Place a book or flat object on the floor and give it a slight forward shove (not too hard, now). Watch the motion and describe what you observe. Explain your observation in your laboratory book in terms of force.

Let's try for a record and do another experiment. Everybody lean up against a wall and try to explain in your laboratory books why the wall does not accelerate. Be careful with your answers; don't say simply, "Because it is attached to the floor" or "Because it is bigger than me." Try to think in terms of the ideas expressed in these last experiments (that is, use the terms *mass, force,* and *acceleration*).

Before we begin to explain exactly what happened in this experiment, let's take time out from our Late Night Snack for a Tasty Nibble . . .

11

Tasty Nibble

To the Student

We must confess a secret . . . force can be a sneaky and even somewhat devious little idea to master—but you will master it.

Given your current understanding of force, if you were walking around looking for forces you might say, "Anytime I see a mass accelerating or decelerating, I know there is a force acting on the mass." (You should keep in mind that a deceleration is just a negative acceleration.) Following are some common examples (consult your laboratory book on the previous home experiment): "I saw someone throw a ball in the air. It quickly came to rest at the top. The ball is a mass and it was decelerating, so a force must have been acting on it." "I saw a car come to a stop. The car is a mass, and it was decelerating. Therefore, there must have been a force acting on it, too."

That part is easy, but consider the following question: What happens when you know there is a force at work but you don't see an acceleration? Let's look at the following example:

A small hedgehog falls from a high-wire to a net below. Now since the hedgehog is a mass and it is accelerating (in this case a positive acceleration), you know it has a force on it, right? (Notice that this sentence is ever so slightly reworded. We can say a mass *has* a force *acting* on it, or shorten it by simply saying a mass *has* a force.)

So far, so good. Let's pretend there is a really big and thick brick wall right in front of a race car (just like you leaning up against the wall in an earlier experiment, right?). When the car tries to accelerate, it cannot go anywhere, of course. You might decide that since this mass is not accelerating, there is no force, even though you know there should be (you wouldn't want to be standing between the car and the wall, would you?). We can address this one easily enough. Just imagine what would happen if the wall were to suddenly disappear. Then the car would accelerate, and you would have your nice, friendly force back again. The wall exerts its own force on the car. (Doesn't this sound a lot like the water's resistive force from before and the force of the wall on you while you were leaning on the wall?) Do you see how easy it is to answer questions when you have the right tools to answer them? That's what physics is all about. Also notice the differences there were among the particular experiments we just performed (cars up against walls, rocks falling in water, you and your classmates leaning against walls) yet how similar the explanations of your observations were. Each experiment could be explained or described by using the words *mass, acceleration,* and *force.* Pretty nice, huh!

Now, it seems that every time we look about we observe a force doing this and a force doing that. An object accelerating here, an object accelerating there. Do you see what happened when Sir Isaac invented the concept of force?

In answering some of his own questions he opened the doors to many other questions; we are still studying some today. For instance, what do we really mean by *mass?* (Oh, well, looks like we may have lots of work to do before answering this one.)

Footnote 15

Look up the word *mass* in an encyclopedia or computer database, and record the definition in your laboratory book.

Let's consider the concept of force in some detail now. This time, think of forces as anything capable of changing another object's state of motion. The forces can be either balanced or unbalanced. If they are balanced, there is no acceleration. In the case of the car and the brick wall, the forces are balanced because the car is not changing the motion of the brick wall, nor is the car accelerating. The brick wall must be applying an equal force on the car. A brick wall applying a force? What? Well, that's exactly right. We call this fact Newton's third law of motion, and say it this way:

"If a force is exerted by one object on a second object, then there must exist an equal and opposite force on the first object by the second object."

To see how Newton's third law works, let's think about just one experiment, okay? When you lean against a wall, the wall "leans" against you—the harder you lean against the wall the harder the wall "leans" against you to hold you there, right? When the rock was released in the water, gravity exerted a force on the rock, causing it to accelerate downward. The water exerted a resistive force upward. Since the water produced a force on the rock that was weaker than the force of gravity, the rock accelerated. These forces were unbalanced. If they had been balanced, the rock would have floated.

Confused? Good. How does anything accelerate? According to Newton's third law, it may seem that everything should be at a standstill. Imagine you are pushing a large block. You know that the block is exerting an equal and opposite force on you; however, there are other forces acting on the block, such as friction and air resistance, that your force on the block overcomes, causing the block to accelerate. This block has an unbalanced force on it just like the rock in the water. Do you see how Newton's third law applies?

These examples show how Newton's third law works, but they also suggest another way to look at forces: when objects are in contact with one another, they exert forces through Newton's third law, and we call these forces "forces of contact," or more simply, "contact forces."

For instance, when you are standing up, you are pushing against Earth and Earth pushes against you—a contact force. Since you know you are applying a force to Earth, yet you're not accelerating into Earth or off Earth, Earth is pushing you back with the same force. (But you wouldn't want somebody to stand on your hands, would you?) Earth and you are just like the car pushing against the wall—contact forces again.

What does all this have to do with our experiment? A lot actually. Back to our . . .

12

Late Night Snack

To the Teacher

You may want to do this as a group activity with a new group physicist leading the activity and directing the follow-up discussion. Then have a classroom discussion about observations and findings.

Step 1:

Fill a glass or small beaker half full with colored water or iced tea (you can also use a small bubble-level) and place it on a table.

Step 2:

Push the glass, beaker, or bubble level just slightly with your hand so that it accelerates. (This may take some practice, so be patient, okay?)

Answer the following questions:

Questions

1. Describe what happens to the water level or the bubble in the bubble level.

2. Using your current knowledge of force and acceleration, explain what you have observed in this activity.

3. Does direction of motion play a role in this experiment?

4. What happens to the water level or bubble in the bubble level when you stop pushing the glass or level (that is, when you remove the force)?

12 ◆ Late Night Snack

To the Student

We have almost the same situation with the rock outside the tank. The rock, accelerating as a result of the force of gravity, in turn "applies a downward force" to the air, while the air resists and applies an upward force to the rock. Following are some questions to answer:

Why does the air apply an upward force?

Why not a sideways force? (You might want to go back and review air resistance and falling objects.)

The rock falling through air accelerates faster because the air resistance is very, very tiny compared to the water resistance. In other words, the rock-in-air must struggle against a weaker kind of wall than the rock-in-water.

Getting the idea now? What happens if the object in the water applies a force downward while the water supplies the same force upward, so that the two forces are balanced?

To answer the question, let's do another activity.

Again your teacher will drop an object into the tank of water, but this time the object will be a small piece of wood or a cork.

Record your observations in your laboratory book.

We observe that the piece of wood or cork floats, but why?

Well, we know that it must be because the forces are balanced; that is, the force of the water on the wood must balance the force of gravity on the wood. The force that the water (or any liquid, for that matter, as it turns out!) applies to objects in the water is called the *buoyant force*.

Let's try another experiment that may help you understand a question raised earlier in the menu. You might recall that we asked how a large metal boat or ship is able to float in water whereas a small pebble simply sinks. Okay, here we go:

Step 1:

Fashion the aluminum foil into a "boat" and place it gently into the tank of water. Observe that the foil floats. Now gently place the large paper clip on the floating aluminum foil and notice that the foil acts as a small boat to carry the paper clip.

Restaurant at the Beginning of the Universe © 1997 Zephyr Press, Tucson, Arizona

Step 2:

With the same piece of aluminum foil, wrap the paper clip as tightly as possible. Return the foil-wrapped paper clip to the water. Does it float now? Why not?

Well, the answer to this one is the *buoyant force*. Buoyant force arises from the total amount of water (or fluid) displaced by an object when it is placed in the water; that is, the more water displaced, the greater the buoyant force acting to prevent the object's sinking. The foil boat carrying the paper clip displaced more water, so the buoyant force was great enough to hold it up. The wrapped paper clip does not displace as much water, so the buoyant force is weaker and not strong enough to prevent the foil and clip from sinking. This is an unbalanced force, right?

So there you have it. Notice that boats and ships have very broad bases to displace as much water as possible, creating enough of a buoyant force to keep them afloat.

Whew! Your brain must be stuffed, what with such a hearty House Specialty, Late Night Snack, not to mention that spicy little Tasty Nibble. Before we take a break, consider the following questions. Oh, here they come.

Questions

At home, perform the following experiment: Fill up a sink with water. Drop in an unopened can of soda, say a cola, and an unopened can of diet cola.

1. Describe what you observed.

2. Try to explain what you observed, using what you have learned so far, including Newton's third law.

3. Is there any relationship between the direction in which a force is acting on an object and the direction in which the object accelerates or moves?

4. Find a picture of a boat or a ship in a book or magazine and draw it in your laboratory book. Identify the parts of the boat, such as the deck, the hull, and so on. Why is the hull shaped as it is?

13

Dessert

Electric Charge and Electricity

To the Teacher

Objectives

Students will describe the direct effects of charged electrostatic objects.

Students will describe the effect of the electrostatic force.

These objectives will provide interest and stimulate curiosity as students learn the theory behind these experiments and activities.

Equipment

several small- to medium-sized (inexpensive) Styrofoam cups
(Do not use the more expensive, thin, coated Styrofoam cups.)

Procedure

Step 1:

Divide the class into groups as usual and have them select new group physicists.

Step 2:

Guide students through the following procedure. Encourage them to explore and experiment.

13 ◆ Dessert

To the Student

Now that you are familiar with the concept of force and can see how various forces act in nature, let's take a look at a completely new force: the force produced by *electric charge*. (Uh-oh, this sounds bad!!)

Footnote 16

Look up the words *electra* and *electric* in a dictionary or encyclopedia. Record these definitions in your laboratory book, as usual, for later reference.

As you have noticed by now, each new concept learned in physics is the foundation upon which other concepts are built. To understand this structure, we are going to dabble a bit in the world of electric charge—just a little bit, though.

As you will learn much later in your study of physics, the concept of electric charge is truly fundamental to the understanding of such phenomena as *electrostatic charge, electricity, magnetism, electromagnetism,* and *light*. Although it sounds somewhat strange, we could not begin to understand the concept of the electric force without having the fundamentals we have discussed up to this point, such as *mass, acceleration,* and *force*. In this context, then, we'll discuss the concepts of electric charge and the electric force.

Step 1:

Each group has been given two Styrofoam cups. You will rub each cup against something to give it a charge. Try rubbing the cups on your hair, your clothing, the carpeting in the room, and so on—be creative!

Restaurant at the Beginning of the Universe © 1997 Zephyr Press, Tucson, Arizona

Step 2:

Place one cup on the table, and hold the other cup ¹/₂ to 1 foot directly above the first cup.

Step 3:

Release the cup, trying to have it fall directly into the first cup. Observe what happens and record your observations in your book.

Step 4:

Draw diagrams of the cups, showing in your diagrams the results of the experiment.

To explain what happened, we say that the act of rubbing the cups against something in effect *charges* the cups with an *electric charge*. If both cups have the same charge, then they repel each other, and the falling cup will not fall directly into the stationary cup.

Questions

1. Describe in your laboratory book what you observed. Did the cups attract or repel?

2. Explain your observations.

3. Was there a sideways force acting on the falling cup?

4. Have you ever walked across a carpet, then touched something and gotten zapped by static electricity? Do you think this experiment is related to your experience? If so, explain.

The Dessert Topping

The Electric Force

To the Student

In this section we incorporate all our previously learned concepts to help explain this new force, the electric force. We recall that while ravenously feasting on House Specialty 1, we learned that perception can differ greatly from reality.

Let's take an imaginary *gastronomic* journey (what's that?) into the world of the very, very, very small, and let's see with our mind's eye what we cannot actually see.

We will begin with an ordinary ruler. If the ruler were placed very, very, very far away and we were told to guess what it was (assuming we didn't know beforehand that it was a ruler), then we would have no hope of making the correct guess, unless, of course, we cheated and used a telescope (or perhaps used someone who has eagle eyes).

Now, if the ruler were moved closer, closer, and closer, its shape would become somewhat distinguishable. In other words, we could see that it was beginning to look like a ruler. Of course, at exactly what distance the object begins to be discernible depends on many things—mostly, the observer's eyesight, right?

Well, from such a distance we might determine that we were actually looking at a ruler, but we probably wouldn't be able to tell what kind of a ruler, that is, whether it is one that measures in meters or in inches. As it moves even closer, however, we might be able to begin to see the actual markings and determine the type of ruler.

Other descriptions might also be possible. We might say, "Hey, this metric ruler is very smooth and straight (or continuous) on all sides; there are no rough or jagged edges."

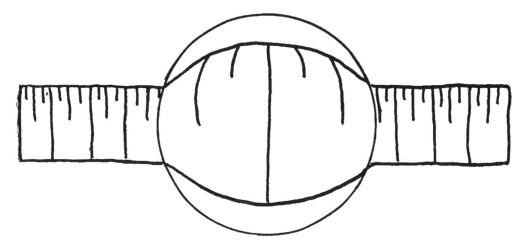

But what if we wanted to look even closer? We could put the ruler under a microscope. We could keep using higher and higher powers on the microscope until a millimeter looked as big as could be.

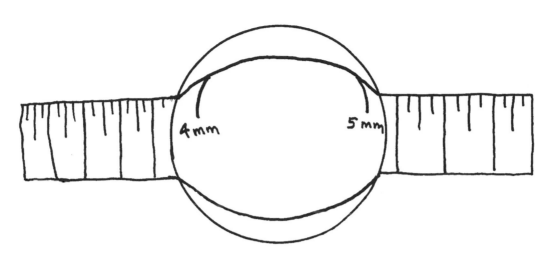

Can we look at it or observe it any more closely than that? Well, we actually can! All that we need is what is called an *electron microscope*. An electron microscope is a superpowerful microscope that lets us see objects closer and better than the best lens microscope. Under the electron microscope the ruler doesn't even look like a ruler anymore. The edge of the ruler looks jagged, like a treacherous mountaintop, because we are able to see each and every fiber of wood that makes up the ruler (if it is a wooden ruler, of course). You might ask, "What would a metal ruler look like?" Well, it would still look jagged because we would see every minuscule imperfection on the ruler's edge.

So our ruler doesn't look so smooth and straight anymore. Perception is indeed quite different from reality, in this case. The next obvious question is, "Can we look even closer?"

We don't have any machines to look through that are more powerful than the electron microscope, but we do have our imaginations—and that's the most powerful machine of all. Curious? Then keep reading . . .

As we increase the magnification on our imaginary microscope, we find there is nothing smooth, straight, or continuous about our ruler at all. It is in fact made up of many billions and billions and billions of tiny little particles called *atoms*. In fact, virtually all matter is made up of atoms—you, the ruler, your books, the water running in rivers, the air, the galaxies, the oceans, and even your teacher! These atoms are strange little things, as we will learn.

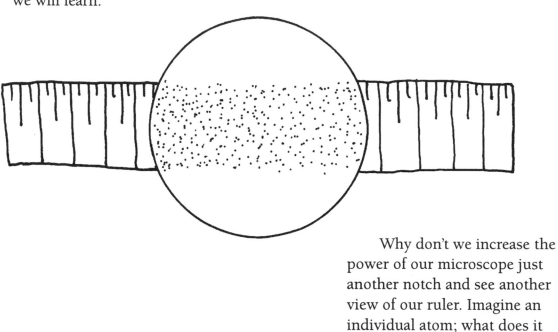

Why don't we increase the power of our microscope just another notch and see another view of our ruler. Imagine an individual atom; what does it look like?

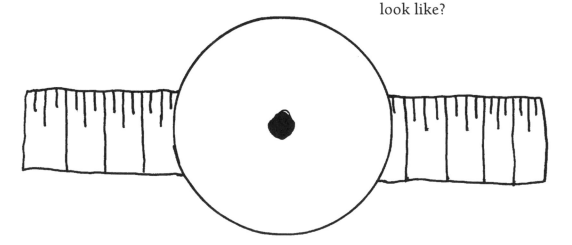

Restaurant at the Beginning of the Universe © 1997 Zephyr Press, Tucson, Arizona

We'll just have to increase the power of our imaginary microscope yet another notch and observe. When we examine the atom this closely, we find that it is actually made up of even smaller particles.

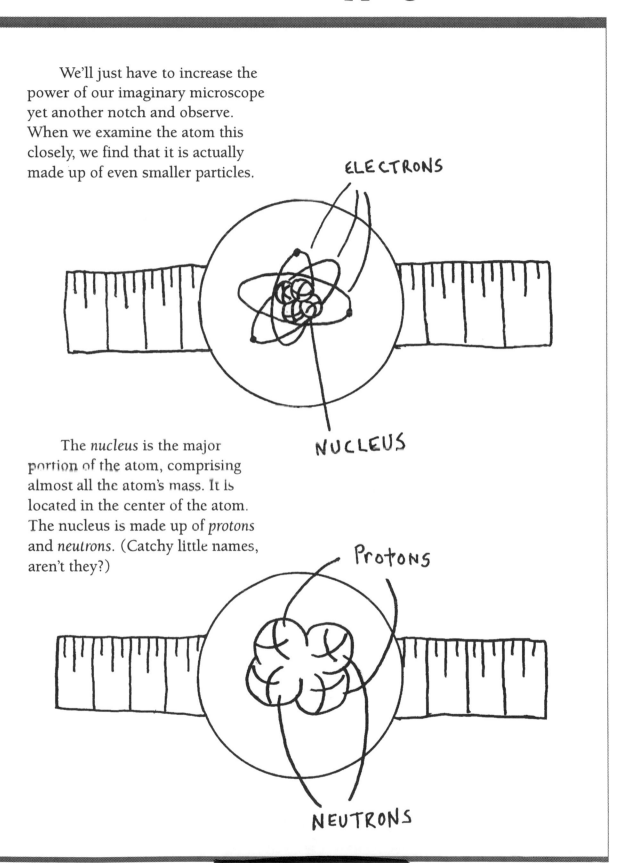

The *nucleus* is the major portion of the atom, comprising almost all the atom's mass. It is located in the center of the atom. The nucleus is made up of *protons* and *neutrons*. (Catchy little names, aren't they?)

The electrons are very, very, very tiny particles that travel around the protons and neutrons. As small as protons and neutrons are (actually, no one has ever actually seen one yet), the electrons are even smaller.

There are many different kinds of atoms. Each kind is distinguishable from another kind by the total number of protons and neutrons it contains. The elements are simply groups of atoms that have the same number of protons and neutrons. (In general, the atom is said to be neutral in charge if the number of electrons is the same as the number of protons, but we'll get to that concept later.)

For example, helium is neutral because it has two protons, two neutrons, and two electrons. All atoms with this structure are called helium atoms; this is the *atomic structure* of helium, and because helium has an atomic structure, it is an element. (This element is used to fill up balloons so that they float in air. Which *raises*—ha, ha—another question: Why do helium balloons float? Think about the buoyant force. Uh-oh, did you forget that?)

You might be thinking that this atomic structure looks like our solar system. The electrons seem to orbit around the nucleus the same way the planets orbit around the Sun. Well, atoms are a little more complicated than that, but for our purposes the solar system idea will work just fine.

There are a few tasty tidbits we need to know concerning the atom before we can get to the really tasty part of the dessert.

Recall what we said much earlier, that is, that all objects have a quantity called *mass*. Now remember the definition of *mass* you looked up in footnote 15. Mass is just some quantity that all objects have in common, and we use units such as *grams* or *kilograms* to describe how much mass an object contains. Since these new particles—protons, neutrons, and electrons—exist, they, too, must have mass. But it so happens that the protons and electrons also have a quantity called the *electric charge*. Just as with mass, no one is exactly sure what charge is, but just as we can measure mass, we can measure the electric charge of a particle. The basic feature is that charge is either *positive* or *negative*, the same way that a light switch is either on or off—nothing in between! It turns out that all protons carry a positive charge and that all electrons carry a negative charge. The neutrons carry no charge and are simply neutral.

14 ◆ The Dessert Topping (continued)

Protons and electrons get along in a special way: like charges repel, and unlike charges attract. Although we do not know exactly what electric charge is, we do know what it does: it creates what is called electric force; it is this force that keeps the atoms intact, much like the gravitational force we saw earlier, which acts between masses only and which is also what keeps our solar system intact. But do not confuse these two forces: the gravitational force between masses is much different from the electrical force between charges.

We can calculate the total charge in an atom simply by adding all the positive and negative charges together. Since helium has two protons and two electrons, we have +2 protons added to -2 electrons = 0 net charge. (It's just like we have two pennies [+2] and buy something with the 2 pennies [-2] we have no more pennies [0], right?) So the helium atom has a net charge of zero, which means it is a *neutral atom.*

Sometimes atoms have a number of protons different from the number of electrons, which causes the atom to have a charge. For example, in the case of an atom with 2 protons and 3 electrons (remember: we don't include the neutrons because they don't have any charge), we determine the charge as follows: +2 protons added to -3 electrons = -1 net charge. So this atom has a charge of -1. Now, that's not so hard, is it? (Just think about saving and then spending pennies!)

You should be getting the idea that not only do protons and electrons have charges, but atoms can have a net charge, as well.

Let's return to our Styrofoam cup activity. But first, remember munching on House Specialty 3: A Piece of the Pi, then having a side order of Archimedes' ideas, then taking a quick peek at the buffet Right or Wrong Triangles? You should have a lot of familiarity with the concept of area. The surface of your Styrofoam cups in your last experiment had an area, right? For example, if you were to cut the cups correctly and lay them flat on a table, you could measure their area easily.

When you rubbed the Styrofoam cups on your hair or your clothing, the atoms on the cups exchanged some electrons. Recall that protons and electrons add up to give an atom a charge. Well, guess what? We can charge the atoms on our Styrofoam cup to obtain a charged cup! When this Styrofoam cup takes on electrons from your hair or clothing, it becomes a charged cup due to the billions of atoms that became charged on its surface area.

Career Note

Someday you will learn that charged atoms must stay on the Styrofoam cup; they cannot go anywhere else. Once you have charged the cup, the charges remain on the cup for a long time.

We told you earlier that the electric force, rather than gravity, holds the atoms together. Gravity keeps us on Earth, it is the force that keeps our solar system together, and it is, no doubt, the force with which we are most familiar. So you may be a little skeptical about this electric force business—you should be!

Instead of the electric force, why can't the force of gravity hold atoms together? That question will be answered a bit later as you continue your quest for answers about the universe you live in.

How do we know that electric charges create a new force all of their own? How can we prove that they do?

Well, we already did!

Remember when you had House Specialty 4 and liked it so much that you even went on to have the Late Night Snack called "Force in the Real World?" You learned that when a mass accelerates, there must be a force acting on it from somewhere.

The Styrofoam cup has a mass, right? We know that it accelerates toward Earth due to gravitational force (it didn't rise into the air and float around when you let go of it, did it?). The question is, What caused it to accelerate away from the top of the cup on the table and fall to the side? A new and different force must be lurking somewhere and—you guessed it—it is the electric force.

If both cups are charged and both cups have the same charge (remember, like charges repel and unlike charges attract) then they will repel each other. This property is exactly what you witnessed in your previous experiment. The charges on the cup caused the cup to accelerate. In fact, you can use this experiment with your friends and family to demonstrate a fundamental force in the universe— the electric force.

House Specialty Five

The Electric Field

To the Student

In the last chapter we told you that charges can attract or repel, depending on whether they are positive or negative. How do the charges "know" another charge is around? Let's snack on this question for a bit. Consider two charges, one positive and the other negative. If the two particles are supposed to attract each other, then they must be "communicating" somehow. By the word *communicating* we mean that they must have some way of letting the other know they are there. Well, they don't do this by shouting at each other, and they don't "talk" like you and me. In fact, they have a very interesting and strange way of communicating . . .

Footnote 17

The word *gedankenexperiment* is German. It means "thought experiment" in English. Thought experiments are exactly what the words imply: experiments that you simply think about, rather than perform with objects and measuring devices. Albert Einstein used this phrase (although he was not the first to do thought experiments). When Einstein was formulating the special, and later the general, theories of relativity, he used thought experiments to arrive at many of his conclusions. In fact, he had no choice because, at the time, the technology didn't exist for him to test his theories.

Arguably one of the most amazing and beautiful scientific discoveries ever, the general theory of relativity, was derived without expensive, complex equipment. Einstein simply thought and imagined and thought and imagined until he arrived at what he believed to be a more accurate description of gravity.

In your school library, you will find many fascinating books on the life of Albert Einstein. Write a paragraph about this quiet and pacifistic scientist.

Restaurant at the Beginning of the Universe © 1997 Zephyr Press, Tucson, Arizona

> ## Career Note
>
> Someday you will learn that the physics of the very small (some of which you are learning about in these chapters) and the physics of the very large (such as general relativity) do not fit together. In other words, each of these disciplines of science, called *quantum mechanics* and *general relativity*, cannot be combined into one theory (at least no one has figured out how to do it; even Einstein couldn't do it). For many, many years scientists have tried to combine these two theories without success. Maybe you are the person to do it! Start thinking about it *now*!

In order to understand the new "language" of these tiny particles, let's do a thought experiment. Imagine that you are very high up, looking down on a field. Instead of a field full of grass and trees and flowers, however, this field is full of little arrows. As you can see, this is no ordinary field; it is special, almost magical.

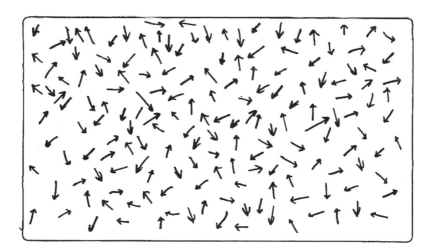

These arrows can go anywhere they choose in the field and they can point in any direction—they are lazy and undisciplined. Whenever the drill sergeant (a proton or electron) comes around, though, they start behaving.

In this field the little arrows *react* to the presence of, let's say, a positive charge (such as the proton), by lining up (like little arrow soldiers) in a starlike formation.

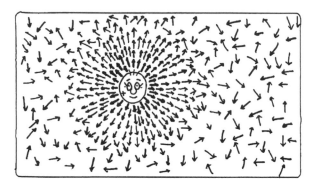

It turns out that all of the arrows will arrange themselves in this fashion whenever they are in the presence of a proton. (Protons make really tough drill sergeants.) If the arrows are far, far away from the proton, then they can point in any direction they choose—they get lazier and lazier the farther they get from the proton. When the proton travels through this field at a constant velocity, it will align all the nearby arrows into the star pattern.

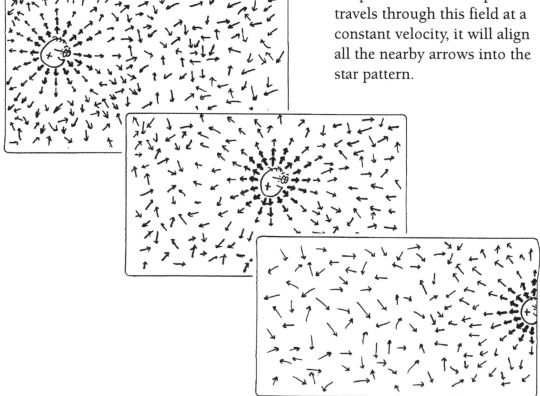

Why doesn't the proton force all the arrows in the field to line up? It can't do that simply because it only has a certain amount of strength, just like a weight lifter, who can lift only so much weight.

The proton can only align the arrows out to a certain distance from its center. What does all this lining up have to do with helping the proton communicate? Well, imagine that the proton wants to know if another proton is in the area. It takes out a spyglass to get a good look at the surrounding area. We expect the proton to be familiar with the star formation it causes; after all, good drill sergeants keep good track of their own troops. But as the proton looks out farther and farther, it notices that all the outlying arrows are pointing in random directions.

No matter which direction the proton looks, it sees that the arrows are not lined up in any special pattern. The drill sergeant proton knows that the only way the faraway arrows can line up is if another proton or an electron is forcing them to do so. The arrow field only responds to positive or negative charges, so a neutron has no effect at all on any of the arrows. Thus the proton concludes that it is the only charged particle in the area. It is a very lonely proton.

If there were another proton nearby, we know that it would straighten up all the lazy arrows, which would be the signal to the spying proton that a friend is nearby.

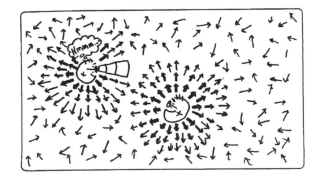

Okay, okay, so now you know how protons communicate—they "alter" or "disturb" the surrounding arrow field and can detect the presence of other protons. You might be thinking, so what? So these protons are able to detect or communicate with other protons, but then what? What do they communicate or "talk" about?

That's easy. As you remember from our discussion about electric charge, like charges repel. The two protons in our example repel each other because the arrows point away from their centers and thus they "push" each other away.

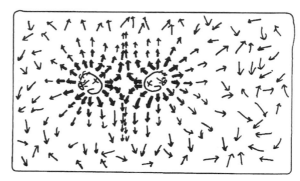

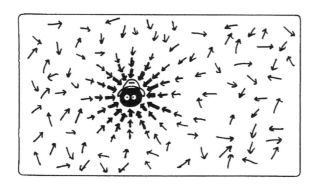

But what happens when a proton and an electron meet? You already know that unlike charges attract, but what do their fields look like? You probably guessed it—the arrows around an electron point toward the electron.

When an electron and proton find each other they attract, or pull toward, each other.

It so happens that protons, electrons, neutrons, atoms, and molecules "live" in this arrow field, except that it's not actually called the *arrow field* but the *electric field*.

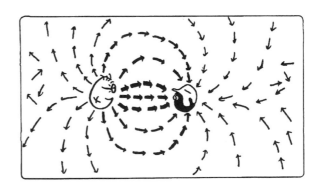

Note

These little arrows don't really exist, so don't look for them, okay? They are what we call a *model*, which is a physical representation of what *may* be happening. (Remember, this is a thought experiment, so use your imagination.) Now, if you really want to impress your friends, tell them this is a *vector field model*. By the way, have you noticed that physicists have really catchy names for everything?

Anyway, you are probably wondering why we use all these little arrows to represent this electric field. We use arrows because they show direction and magnitude, that is, the strength, of the electric field.

Each arrow points in the direction of the electric field surrounding the particle, and the thickness of the arrow represents the field's magnitude. Notice that the arrows close to the charge are thicker than the ones farther away. That's because the electric field is strongest closer to the proton or electron (the drill sergeant can keep a good eye on those cadets that are nearest him).

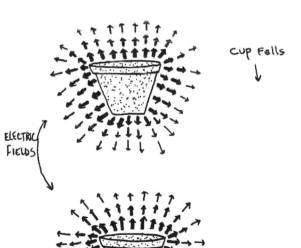

How does this knowledge of the electric field relate to electric charge? Good question. Let's take a look at the experiment with the charged styrofoam cups. Recall that when the cups were charged with the same charge they repelled each other.

Each charged particle in the cup had an electric field surrounding it. All the charges in each cup added up to create an electric field around each cup.

If both cups have the same charge, then their electric fields will point against each other, and they will repel each other.

Falls

DEFLECTS

Restaurant at the Beginning of the Universe © 1997 Zephyr Press, Tucson, Arizona

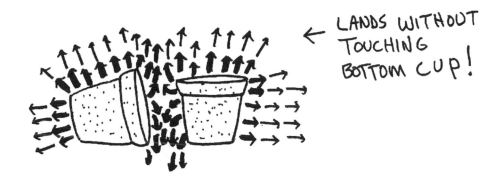

So you see that charges communicate through their electric fields. The cups didn't even have to touch! It was the interaction of their electric fields that caused the top cup to deflect.

Footnote 18

The French physicist Charles A. de Coulomb (1736–1806) discovered the relationship between electric force and electric charge. The mathematical relationship he discovered to describe this force is called Coulomb's law. Research this scientist. Write a brief paragraph (with sketches) describing the device he invented and used to discover his law.

Career Note

As you pursue your career in physics you will run across a device called the *Cavendish balance*. It is very similar to Coulomb's device except it explores the concept of gravitational attraction. The interesting feature of the Cavendish balance is that it uses metal balls that move because of gravitational attraction.

15 ◆ House Specialty Five (continued)

Questions

1. Sketch the electric field arrows of two electrons. Do these particles repel or attract each other?

2. Sketch the electric field arrows for a neutron. Describe this field in words.

3. Does a proton repel or attract a neutron? Explain.

4. Does an electron repel or attract a neutron? Explain.

5. In the cup experiment, what happens when only one cup is charged? Why?

6. Are there any similarities between the cup experiment and the device used by Coulomb?

7. Why doesn't the neutron affect the electric arrow field?

8. Would a neutral atom affect the arrow field? How about a charged atom?

The electric field has a very close friend. You are already familiar with this friend, the magnetic field, but up until now you probably haven't realized they even knew each other. Open your menu and take a look at a very "attractive" specialty . . .

16

House Specialty Six

Magnetism

To the Teacher

Objective

Students will observe magnetic field patterns.

Equipment

This demonstration can be done either as a class or in small groups, depending on availability of equipment.

magnet, preferably a bar magnet

iron filings

paper

Procedure

Step 1:

Place the magnet on a table and cover it with a sheet of blank paper.

Step 2:

Liberally sprinkle the iron filings on the paper over the magnet while gently tapping the paper with your hand to "jiggle" the filings a bit.

Step 3:

Guide students through the procedure.

16 ◆ House Specialty Six

To the Student

Do you have refrigerator magnets? Or maybe a bar or horseshoe magnet? Have you ever used a magnet to pick up paper clips or other pieces of metal? Why do magnets "stick" to a refrigerator? These questions are all good; we're going to answer them in this delicious House Specialty.

Surrounding any magnet is another little arrow field called the *magnetic field*. In the following activity we're going to get a firsthand look at the magnetic field's pattern.

Step 1:

Your teacher has sprinkled iron filings over a magnet. In your own words, describe what happened.

Step 2:

In your laboratory book, sketch the pattern formed by the iron filings.

Questions

1. List and explain the similarities and differences between the patterns in this experiment and those in the electric field.

2. What do you think is causing the iron filings to form the pattern? Be specific.

Scientists describe the space around a permanent magnet, such as the one used in this experiment, as the *location of a magnetic field,* just as the space around a charged object is the *location of an electric field.* Again we use the model of little arrows to represent this new field.

16 ◆ House Specialty Six (continued)

Some of you may have answered question 2 by saying something like the following:

There are little particles, similar to protons and electrons, that create magnetic fields around themselves. One of these particles is positive and its field is directed outward, while the other is negative and its field is directed inward. If many of the positive particles somehow wind up at one end of the bar while the negative particles are at the other end, then the field they produce should look similar to the electric field of two oppositely charged electric particles.

This response would have been an outstanding answer to question 2; however, it is wrong. For more than sixty years physicists have speculated about the existence of particles such as these (if you want to be very technical, they are called *magnetic monopoles*—another cool name, isn't it?). These tiny particles would be just like the proton and electron except they would carry a single north or single south magnetic pole, just as Earth does; however, no such particles have ever been found despite many attempts. The magnetic field of the bar magnet isn't made by magnetic charges, but rather—you'll never believe it—by electrical charges! Let's see how this works . . .

We have talked a great deal about electrical charges, the proton and electron, and some of their properties. One of the most interesting properties of charges occurs when they move at a constant velocity.

André-Marie Ampère (1775–1836) discovered that when a proton or electron (or any electrically charged particle) moves at a constant speed, it creates a magnetic field . . . just like that!

Okay, okay, you're skeptical, aren't you? That's good. We'll prove it to you in the next activity . . .

To The Teacher

Objective

Students will observe how a compass can be used to detect magnetic fields.

Equipment

directional compasses

magnets

Procedure

Step 1:

Move the compass around the magnet to demonstrate the compass's response to magnetic fields.

Step 2:

Guide students through the following procedure.

16 ◆ House Specialty Six

To the Student

Do you know what electricity is? It is the motion of electrons through wires that creates the electricity you use to turn on a light or any other electrical object. That's why electrical objects (say, for instance, your television set) have cords, with metal wires wrapped in protective insulation, connecting them to an outlet.

It is important that you know how electricity works because there is a connection between two of the statements we just made:

1. Electricity is made by electrons moving through wires.

2. A moving charge creates a magnetic field.

If electrons are moving through a wire, they must create a magnetic field around the wire!

What happened when your teacher placed the compass by the bar magnet? The compass responded to the field around it by pointing either toward or away from the magnet, depending on the pole of the magnet. Now you should be convinced that a compass can detect a magnetic field, no matter where that field is.

> ### Career Note
> Someday you will learn that they don't actually move, but for our purposes, we will use this term.

> ### Career Note
> Someday you will learn why only some objects can be magnetized. Also, magnets are magnets because of the special way that electric charges move, but that's stuff you'll have to learn about as you continue your career!

Restaurant at the Beginning of the Universe © 1997 Zephyr Press, Tucson, Arizona

Footnote 19

The English scientist Michael Faraday (1791–1867) investigated many topics in electricity and magnetism. His laboratory books (just like the one you have) contained lots of neat diagrams and some equations!

Much of his thoughts about physics were purely intuitive. Read a book about this interesting scientist and write a brief paragraph about him in your laboratory book. Also look up the word *intuitive* in the dictionary. Write the definition in your laboratory book. Are you intuitive?

Now let's see how we might create magnetism in our next activity . . .

To the Teacher

Objective

Students will observe the relationship between moving charges and the magnetic field such charges must create.

Equipment

about 1 to 2 feet of thin copper wire

two to three 1.5-volt, D-size batteries

a piece of cardboard, just thick enough to be rigid while holding one end

directional compass

iron filings

ring stand and clamp

After reading the procedure, feel free to improvise as necessary, depending on the availability of equipment. Extremism in the pursuit of physics experiments is no vice!

Procedure

Step 1:

Poke two holes, just large enough for the copper wire to fit through, into the cardboard.

Step 2:

Insert the wire through the holes and affix the cardboard to the clamp and ring stand as shown in the sketch in the student section.

Step 3:

Connect the batteries. Do not leave the batteries connected for long. The batteries will die very quickly because there is no resistor in the circuit, but a resistor isn't necessary as long as the batteries are disconnected before and immediately after the demonstration.

Step 4:

Place the directional compass at various locations on the platform and observe the compass's response. (You may need to reposition the wire and the compass to get the best results.) If you do not have a directional compass, try placing iron filings on the platform. Tap the platform gently to align the flings. Be patient; this may take practice.

Step 5:

Lead the class discussion.

16 ◆ House Specialty Six

To the Student

Your teacher has set up the following experiment. The wire is connected to the battery. This connection completes a circuit and causes a current to flow. Electrons are now "moving" through the wire.

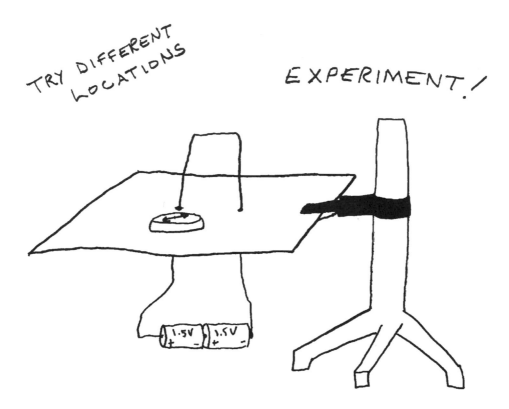

We told you that there should be a magnetic field around the wire when there is a current. When your teacher placed the compass or the iron filings near the wire, what did you observe?

Questions

1. In this experiment, your teacher used a few 1.5-volt batteries. Explain in your own words what the magnetic field would do if a 10-volt battery were used. A 100-volt battery? Make sketches to accompany your explanations.

2. What happens when the wires are disconnected from the battery?

Restaurant at the Beginning of the Universe © 1997 Zephyr Press, Tucson, Arizona

Breath Mint after House Specialty Six

Magnetic Fields Can Affect Charges!

To the Teacher

Objective

Students will observe the relationship between a moving magnetic field and its effect on charges.

Equipment

about 1 to 2 feet of thin copper wire

two or three 1.5-volt, D-size batteries

a piece of cardboard, just thick enough to be rigid while holding one end

directional compass

ring stand and clamp

bar magnet (the stronger the better)

Procedure

Step 1:

Disconnect the battery if it is still connected.

Step 2:

Place the compass on the cardboard next to one of the wires.

Step 3:

Connect the ends of the copper wire.

Step 4:

Wave the bar magnet over the copper wire. Ensure that the magnet is not affecting the compass (keep it as far away from the compass and as close to the wire as possible).

Step 5:

Guide students through the following discussion.

BAR MAGNET

copper wire

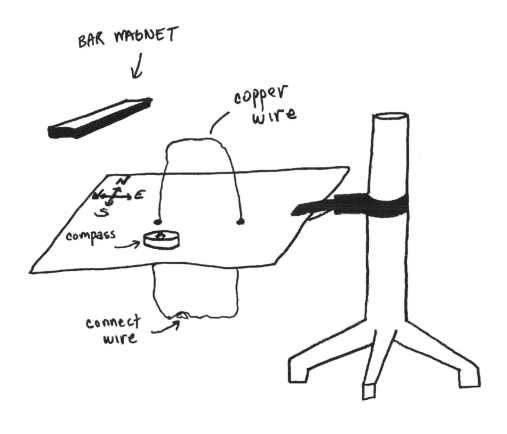

compass

connect wire

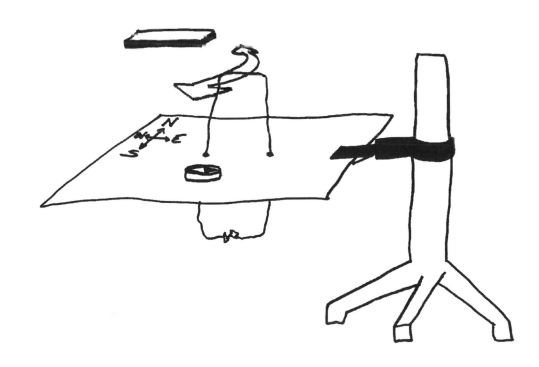

17 ◆ Breath Mint after House Specialty Six

To the Student

You have seen that when an electric charge moves, it creates a magnetic field. But did you know that the reverse is also true? When a magnetic field moves by a stationary charge, it will cause the charge to move. Are you skeptical? You should be! Let's prove it . . .

Your teacher disconnected the wire from the battery, so you know there is no electricity, so no moving charges, so no magnetic field. But what happened to the compass when your teacher waved the magnet by the wire? We'll tell you. The moving magnetic field caused the charges in the wire to move. When the charges began moving within the wire, they created a magnetic field around the wire. The magnetic field around the wire caused the compass to deflect.

Let's sum it all up: When an electric charge moves, it creates a magnetic field. When a magnetic field goes by an electric charge, it causes the charge to move.

Have we forgotten something? Don't you feel as though something is missing from these pages on magnetism? Something is. Previously, when we were discussing the electric field, we used arrows to create a very simple and elegant model of that field. But where are the arrows that represent the magnetic field? If we use little arrows to describe the magnitude and direction of the *electric field,* then why not use them to describe the strength and direction of the *magnetic field?* Hey, that's not a bad idea! Let's try it . . .

Return to your thought-experiment state of mind and imagine another field full of lazy, undisciplined arrows.

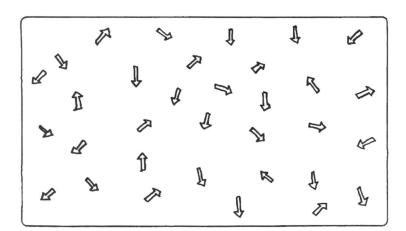

These arrows look a little different from the lazy arrows of the electric field, however, because whenever a charged particle moves through this field, the arrows respond in a slightly different way. To see what they do let's put an electron in this field and give it a little shove so that it has a nice constant velocity out of the page toward you . . .

One . . .

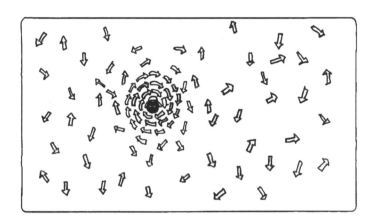

Two . . .

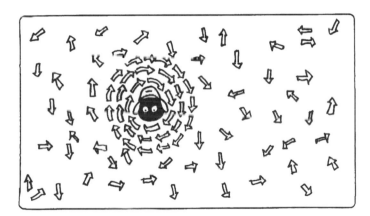

Three . . .

Whoa, Nelly! These arrows don't point inward or outward like the electric field arrows. They point sideways and form circles around the particle. Why? Well, these arrows will take orders only from a charged particle that is moving with a constant velocity. Whenever a proton or electron or charged atom (by the way, a charged atom is called an *ion*) is moving in this manner, it will cause these special arrows to form circles around it. Oh, can you guess what the arrows might do in the presence of a positively charged particle such as a proton? You guessed it . . .

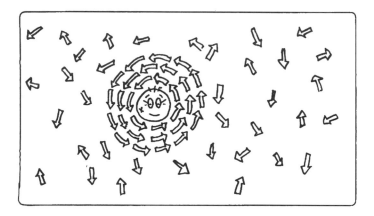

They change direction! Pretty neat, huh? Okay, so the next step is to combine what we already know about the electric field with what we just learned about the magnetic field. You know that a charged particle, moving or not, has to have an electric field around it, so let's take a look at both fields together.

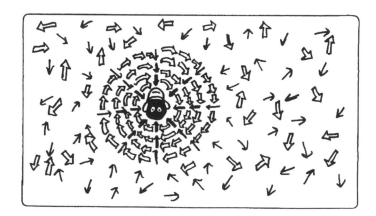

Voila!

The electric and magnetic arrows appear to be at right angles to each other. They are perpendicular, or at 90-degree angles.

Whenever you have an electric field arrow pointing in some direction, the magnetic field arrow will look like this:

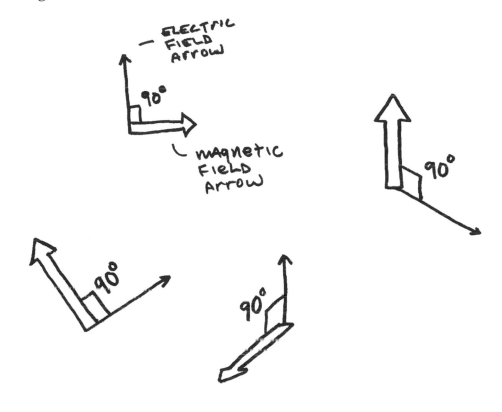

But never like this:

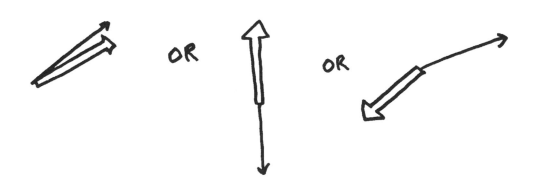

So what is the point? Why bother? Who cares? Well, just hold your horses because we're not done yet. There is a major aspect to all this thought experimenting (is your brain getting pooped yet?) that we have not mentioned so far, so let's talk about it now.

Imagine that you have a cylinder. This cylinder is not hollow, however. This cylinder is solid through and through. You know that we're not going to let you off the hook that easily . . . something is afoot. This cylinder is special because, as it was being manufactured by some crazy scientists, they put arrows inside of it. What? Okay, let's imagine that we take a knife (if you want to use cool words and phrases like physicists do, call the knife a *carefully crafted molecule separating utensil*) and cut the cylinder right through the middle so that we can take a peek at the arrows inside . . .

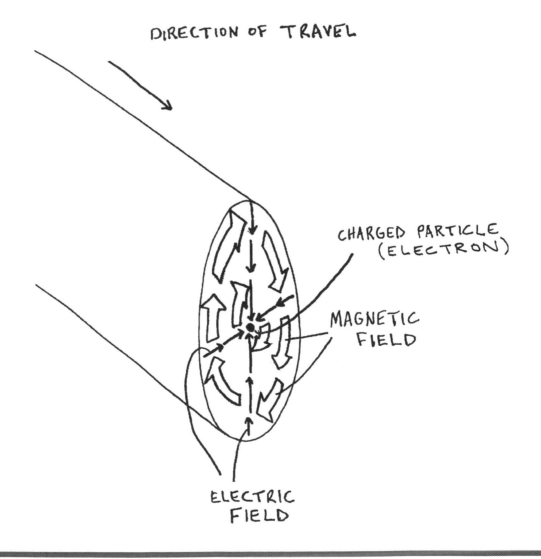

DIRECTION OF TRAVEL

CHARGED PARTICLE (ELECTRON)

MAGNETIC FIELD

ELECTRIC FIELD

Hey! These arrows look like the electric and magnetic field arrows for a positively charged particle! The neat scientists must want us to know that no matter which way we cut the cylinder, we will find these arrows.

Yes! We do see more arrows! Getting the idea? No matter how we cut the cylinder, the arrows have the same pattern. You see, up until now we have shown you the electric and magnetic fields as they would appear in two dimensions. We have only shown you a slice of the fields (sometimes that's the only way to illustrate an idea). Actually, in the real world, the fields more closely resemble the cylinder shape. That is, a charged, moving particle has an electric and magnetic field that completely surrounds it like a cylinder.

You have probably already figured out that as we get farther and farther away from the particle (the center of the ball), the fields get weaker and weaker, just as they did in our two-dimensional models, or "slices."

This stuff is important because we need to understand the three-dimensional model before we can truly understand what really happened in the previous wire experiment.

You see, when billions and billions of charged particles such as electrons move with constant velocity through the wire, they are so close together that they behave as though they were a continuous line of charge. You know that an electron has a negative charge and that when it moves with a constant velocity, it creates a magnetic field. Now imagine taking an electron by the ears and stretching it out like a spaghetti noodle:

Now, this is a line of negative charge, sort of. So the magnetic field around the line (the wire in this case) becomes magnetic field lines.

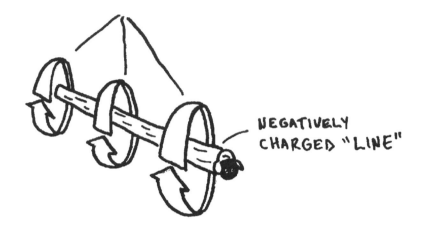

MAGNETIC FIELD "LINE"

NEGATIVELY CHARGED "LINE"

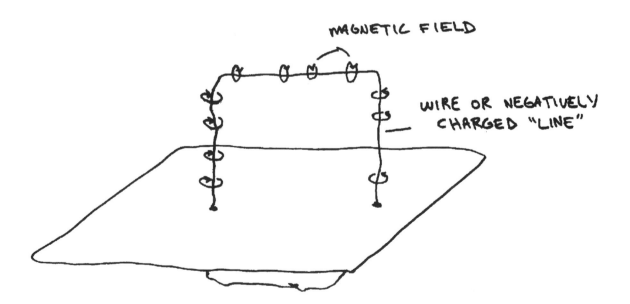

MAGNETIC FIELD

WIRE OR NEGATIVELY CHARGED "LINE"

So no matter where you put the compass, it will always detect the magnetic field line around the wire.

Restaurant at the Beginning of the Universe © 1997 Zephyr Press, Tucson, Arizona

Footnote 20

In 1820 a high school teacher was giving a physics demonstration to his students. He performed *exactly* the same experiment you did with the wire and compass. His name was Hans Christian Oersted and he immediately discovered, just as you did, that there is a direct connection between electric current and magnetism. The only difference is that he was the very first person to notice it.

Write a paragraph in your laboratory book about Oersted and his discovery. You should find that something amazing happened right after his discovery. What was it? Hint: Many inventions occurred because of this discovery!

Do you see why we need to use three dimensions to understand the wire experiment? The magnetic field surrounds the wire. If we were to draw this field in only two dimensions, we wouldn't have a very complete picture:

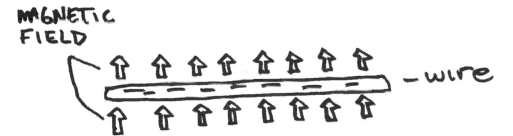

Notice that this diagram shows only a slice.

The interactions between current, electric fields, and magnetic fields have many, many properties that are too numerous to discuss in detail here. A few properties are *inductance, capacitance, current loops, solenoids, toroids,* and *cathode ray tubes* (which are in your television set). All these strange things are possible because magnetic fields create a force on electric charges, and in turn electric fields can alter magnetic fields, and so on and so forth.

Finally we are getting down to the nitty gritty. Actually, not just the nitty gritty but the nitty, nitty, nitty gritty. We are going to combine the following three ideas—our three-dimensional model of electric and magnetic fields, the concept of acceleration, and the concept of the 90-degree angle between electric and magnetic fields—into one beautiful and simple result. Open your menu to the final . . .

Dainty Morsel after House Specialty Six and Right before the Breath Mint

Making Waves

To the Student

We have prattled on and on about the properties of charged particles moving at constant velocities. You know that whether a charge is moving or not it has an electric field. And once it moves at a constant velocity, it creates a nifty little magnetic field around itself. We showed you what these fields look like and we had you perform some experiments that illustrated their effects. In this Dainty Morsel, we show you what happens when these particles move with a changing velocity or acceleration.

Imagine (we say that an awful lot, don't we?) that you have a basketball floating on the surface of a pool. (It certainly wouldn't be "floating" on the bottom of the pool, now, would it?)

If you were to move the ball, you know what would happen, don't you?

It would make waves on the surface of the water, of course Well, it so happens that when a charge accelerates, and only when it accelerates, it creates a wave. What kind of wave, you ask? Good question. It causes the electric and magnetic fields to "wave." This wave is called—you guessed it—an electromagnetic wave.

The electromagnetic wave is very similar to the water waves with which you are already familiar; however, there are a few important differences. The electric and magnetic parts of the electromagnetic waves are at right angles to each other *and* they wave in three dimensions! What? Come again? How so? What does that mean? What would this wave look like? Good questions. Let's find out.

We can't actually show you what these waves look like as they spread out from the particle because they would be very difficult, if not impossible, to draw. When visualizing these waves, remember the sphere model we talked about. That model belongs to you now and is at the command of your imagination whenever you want to bring it out. So keep in mind that these waves are going off in all directions. This is very different from the basketball-in-a-pool wave, since those waves can only be found on the

Now, we know that the fields must be at right angles to each other and that they move away from the particle in every direction. Given these clues, let's take a snapshot or slice of these waves and see what they might look like. We'll begin by looking only at the electric field waves:

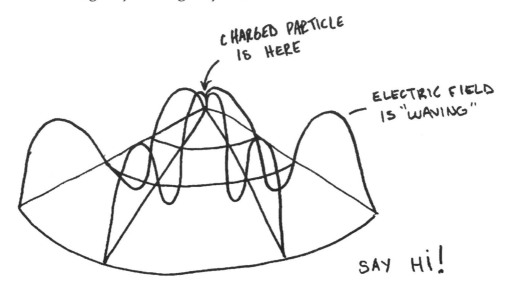

Notice that the waves all begin at the location of the particle, just like the water waves begin at the location of the basketball and move away. Now, if the magnetic field is also waving, and it certainly is, then it should look slightly different because it is at a right angle to the electric field wave. In fact, the magnetic waves move right along with the electric waves and look like this:

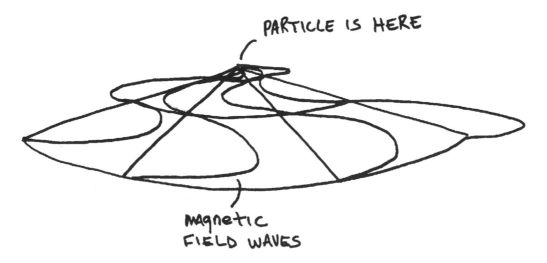

Looks a little strange, doesn't it? Well, it gets even stranger. Nature has decided that there can never be a magnetic wave without its partner, an electric wave. The reverse is also true—there can never be an electric wave without its buddy, a magnetic wave. The two are always together, no matter what.

In other words, there is no such thing as a magnetic wave or an electric wave—only electromagnetic waves. So let's take a look at these waves when we combine them. We'll shade in the electric waves so you can see them more easily:

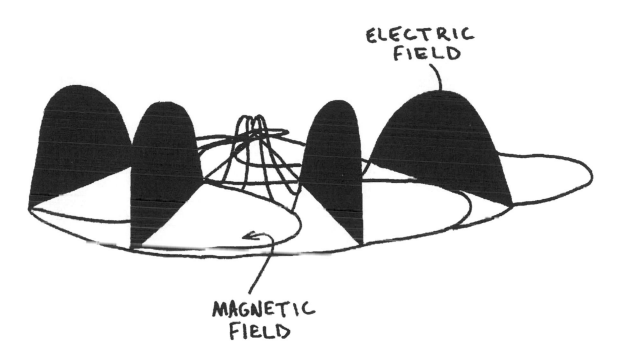

Notice that whenever the electric field is at a peak, the magnetic field is, as well, and whenever one is at a low point, so is the other.

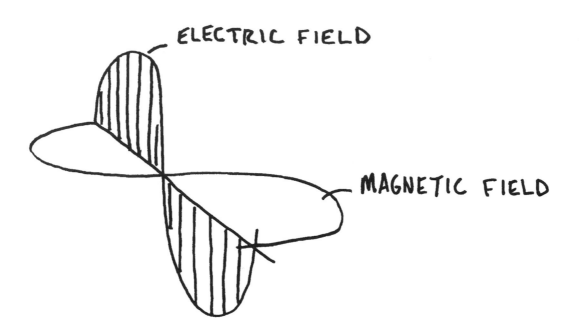

ELECTRIC FIELD

MAGNETIC FIELD

All electromagnetic waves travel at the same speed, the speed of light, which is 299,000,000 meters per second. Now, that's fast!

Career Note

Someday you will find out why nothing in the universe can travel faster than the speed of light. It is truly the cosmic speed limit!

Footnote 21

James Clerk Maxwell (1831–79) was a Scottish scientist who discovered electromagnetic waves and calculated their speed. On the night of his discovery, he was walking through the park with his girlfriend, whom he would later marry, when he asked her how she would feel to know that he was the only person in the world who knew what light was! Imagine that. Well, James *was* the only person to know at the time. In your laboratory books, write a brief paragraph about James and his discovery.

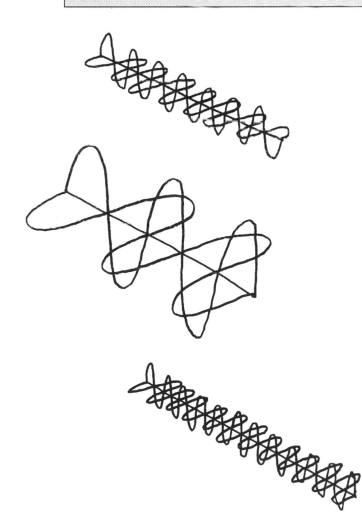

Before eating the last bite of the Dainty Morsel let's talk a little more about waves.

Waves, all waves, not just the electromagnetic kind, have many disguises they can wear. You see, radio waves are actually electromagnetic waves; so are microwaves (yes, the kind you will find in your microwave at home), gamma rays, x-rays, ultraviolet waves, infrared waves, and even the light we use to see is an electromagnetic wave. How can electromagnetic waves do all of this? Well, sometimes the waves can wave very quickly.

Other times they just take their time.

18 ◆ Dainty Morsel *(continued)*

The rate at which the wave waves (physicists call these movements *oscillations*) is called the *frequency*. The higher the frequency, the more energy the wave has. Electromagnetic waves with very high frequencies might be gamma rays or x-rays. When electromagnetic waves take their time and have low frequencies, they might be infrared or radio waves. The light that helps us to see lies somewhere in between.

Waves also have a size; that is, they might crest high or low, like this:

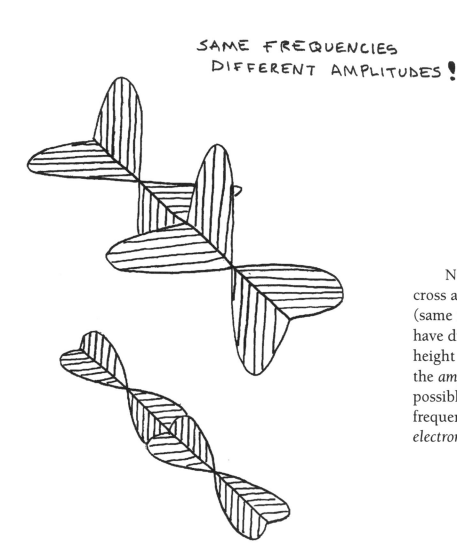

SAME FREQUENCIES
DIFFERENT AMPLITUDES!

Notice that the waves cross at the same points (same frequency), but they have different heights (the height of the wave is called the *amplitude*). We call all the possible combinations of frequency the *spectrum*—the *electromagnetic* spectrum.

19

The Breath Mint Right after the Dainty Morsel

There are numerous experiments and things to learn about electromagnetism, such as optics, refraction, reflection, and interference. We simply cannot cover them all.

Someday you will learn that light can behave as though it were a particle instead of a wave. Or that it is the speed of the electromagnetic wave that is so important in explaining why time slows down at very high velocities, why your mass gets bigger and bigger while your length will get shorter. Remember, don't be afraid to explore all the things we've talked about in greater detail.

Conclusion

Don't Forget to Leave the Tip!

We hope you agree that *The Restaurant at the Beginning of the Universe* has the best menu this side of the cosmos, from the main course right through to the dessert and topping. Grab a toothpick, sit back, and relax for a moment; reflect on all the things you have learned. We know that science, and physics especially, is often taught in such a way that much of the fun and wonderment is left out. We think our new menu is exciting and just plain fun, and we hope you do, too.

Oh. Don't forget to leave a tip . . .

Bibliography

Ball, W., and W. Rouse. 1960. *A Short Account of the History of Mathematics*. New York: Dover.

Bruetsch, Anne. 1995. *Multiple Intelligences Lesson Plan Book*. Tucson, Ariz.: Zephyr Press.

Gardner, Robert. 1986. *Ideas for Science Projects*. Chicago: Franklin Watts.

―――. 1989. *More Ideas for Science Projects*. Chicago: Franklin Watts.

Halliday, David, Robert Resnick, and Kenneth S. Krane. 1992a. *Physics*. Vol. 1. 4th ed. New York: John Wiley.

―――. 1992b. *Physics*. Vol. 2. 4th ed. New York: John Wiley.

Hawking, Steven. 1990. *A Brief History of Time*. New York: Bantam.

Hewitt, Paul G. 1993. *Conceptual Physics*. 7th ed. New York: HarperCollins College.

Kline, Morris. 1959. *Mathematics and the Physical World*. New York: Dover.

Krauss, Lawrence M. 1993. *Fear of Physics: A Guide for the Perplexed*. New York: Basic.

Larson, Hostetler. 1989a. *College Algebra*. Toronto, D.C.: Heath.

―――. 1989b. *Trigonometry*. Toronto, D.C.: Heath.

Mandell, Muriel. 1968. *Physics Experiments for Children*. Mineola, N.Y.: Dover.

March, Robert H. 1970. *Physics for Poets*. New York: McGraw-Hill.

Margulies, Nancy. 1991. *Mapping Inner Space*. Tucson, Ariz.: Zephyr Press.

Marshall Cavendish Corporation. 1989. *Science in Action: Experiments in Physics*. New York: Marshall Cavendish Corporation.

Pappas, Theoni. 1989. *The Joy of Mathematics*. San Carlos, Calif.: Wide World, Tetra.

Stangl, Jean. 1994. *Science Toolbox: Making and Using the Tools of Science*. 2nd ed. Blue Ridge Summit, Pa.: TAB.

Van Cleave, Janice. 1991. *Physics for Every Kid*. New York: John Wiley.

Vermillion, Robert E. 1991. *Projects and Investigations: The Practice of Physics*. New York: Macmillan.

Walker, Jearl. 1977. *The Flying Circus of Physics with Answers*. New York: John Wiley.

Wright, Esmond. 1984. *History of the World*. New York: Bonanza.

Issue 1

October 1996

Cafe Universe *Times*

All the Food That's Fit to Eat

Galileo Refutes Aristotle!

In a startling revelation, Galileo Galilei, professor of mathematics at the University of Pisa, refutes and annoys the followers of Aristotle. In his newly published work *The Dialogue*, Galileo discusses the two leading theories of the order of the universe: the Ptolemaic and Copernican

Ancient Documents Reveal Gravity's Mystery

systems. Proponents of Aristotle's worldview are "completely befuddled and certainly annoyed," says a student of Professor Galilei, Mr. Enzio Aguto, who is studying mathematics and philosophy at the University of Pisa. Galileo supports the Copernican scheme, wherein Earth is not the center of the universe. "This theory has some serious shortcomings," claims another critic. "In fact, it's not even written in scholarly Latin, but in Italian.
    Imagine that!"

As is well known, two objects of the same weight fall at the same rate; when they are released simultaneously from the same height, they reach the ground at the same time. As is also well known, heavier objects fall faster and thus arrive at the ground sooner. However, newly found documents contradict this theory and indicate that objects of different weights fall at the same rate! The new theory is put forth by Professor Galileo Galilei.

Demonstration Set for Tomorrow Morning

Professor Galilei will give a demonstration of his theory tomorrow morning at the Tower of Pisa at 8:00 A.M. Those planning to see the demonstration should arrive early, as we are expecting quite a crowd.

Parallax Method Used to Determine the Distance to the Stars

A simple experiment shows how to use the parallax method to determine the distance to the stars. Here's how it goes: Look at a table or chair in a room, keeping track of all the other objects in the room in relation to the table or chair. Now walk back and forth in a straight line some distance in front of the table or chair. Notice that the chair or table seems to move in relation to the background. The table or chair is said to have undergone a *parallax shift*.

Now imagine observing from Earth a single star in relation to all the background stars. As Earth revolves around the Sun, the star appears to shift in relation to the background: a parallax shift!

This shift is now used to calculate the distance from Earth to the star.

(This system works only for stars that are relatively close to Earth and in cases where the background stars do not appear to move since they are much farther away.)

Parallax Exercise

Look up the word *parallax* and write it in your lab book.

Look up the distance from Earth to a few stars (include the north star).

Time Under Question as Scientists Ponder Its Meaning

As the controversy over Professor Galilei's recently published book grows, the concept of time again comes under scrutiny. Periodic flooding of the Nile River in Egypt convinces some that time must have some importance in determining the nature of humankind.

Although not accepted by all, the concept of time has thus divided the scientific community. "It's just another empty way to attack Aristotle," claims Ms. Maria deLillo, a student of philosophy at the University of Pisa. "Maybe not," says Mr. Carrado Demarco, a student in the same class. "It must be possible to count time just as we count money; for instance, we count our heartbeats and doesn't this give us a sense of rhythm?"

As Professor Galilei remarks, "I can see that this argument will be going on long after I'm gone. Looks like I've started something. Oh, well. You'll have to excuse me; I have papers to grade."

Early Greek Philosophers Establish Scientific Method

Recent investigations suggest that the great natural philosophers (or scientists) were speculating about the structure of the universe as far back as 2500 years ago! The investigations have unearthed such names as Thales, Pythagoras, Philolaus, Socrates, Plato, Eudoxus, Hypatia and, of course, Aristotle.

Philosopher Exercise

In your laboratory book, write a brief biography of each of these philosophers. Include the approximate year each was born, the subjects of their studies, and any writings.

Recording Moon Phases Suggests that the Moon Revolves around Earth

An interesting experiment suggests that the Moon revolves around Earth. Simply note the date, time of day, and phase and position of the Moon. For two to three weeks, each evening just at sunset, record the position of the Moon in relation to a building, tree, mountain, or other fixed object, and its phase. Note that, as the Moon moves farther away from the Sun, it becomes a full Moon. Explain why this experiment proves that the Moon revolves around Earth?

According to Carlo Fortunato, assistant and student of Professor Galilei, "This experiment is amazing! And it is so simple to see, I'm amazed it took so long to see this." In contrast, the critics of Professor Galilei say that this is just another trick to support the Copernican scheme without proof. Professor Enrico Alonso, professor of history, states, "Again we see Aristotle is under attack with frivolous and vacuous arguments. It is best to continue with what we know already."

When interviewed, Professor Galilei says simply, "I guess we'll just have to wait and see, but I have no doubts time will prove the theory correct."

New Words Introduced by the Dialogue

New words have now been introduced into the scientific vocabulary through Professor Galilei's new book. Such words as *time, momentum, impetus,* and *inertia* have now become popular among the students of Natural Philosophy.

Great Scientific Minds Meet

In an attempt to promote the new ideas being introduced by many natural philosophers and scientists, Johannes Kepler is calling a conference. Earlier this year, Kepler extracted three fundamental rules of the motion of the planets based upon the observations of Tycho Brahe. Kepler is convinced that if scientists and philosophers such as Galileo and Rene Descarte could discuss their ideas, the world of science would be advanced.

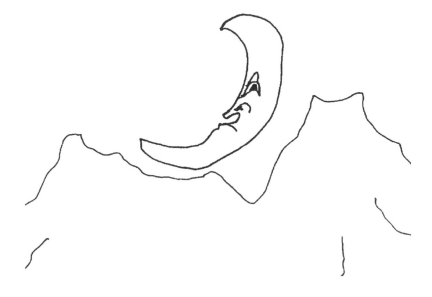

New Way to Express Large Numbers

In a great new way, very large numbers such as—

1.600000000000000000000000
000000000000000000000000000
000000000000000000000000000
0000000000000000000000000

may be written in what is to be called *scientific notation* as 1.6 x 10^{102}. Let's see how this notation works. If 10^2 is 10 x 10 or 100, then 10^3 must be 10 x 10 x 10 or 1000. See the pattern? Just count the zeros! 1.6 x 10^2 is 1.6 x 100 or 160.

Thus, for the very large number above we have 102 zeros and we write it as 1.6 x 10^{102}!

Pascal Discovers a Number Triangle

Blaise Pascal, a French mathematician, discovered a useful number triangle that we are calling Pascal's triangle.

The first and last number of each row is 1, and numbers in between are sums of the two numbers immediately above:

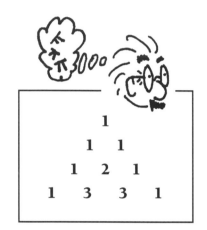

```
        1
      1   1
    1   2   1
  1   3   3   1
```

Note that the 2 is derived by adding the 1s to the right and left above it and that the 3s are derived by adding the 1s and 2s to the right and left above each. Pascal found that these numbers play a special role in algebra. He refused to answer exactly what role these numbers play, but he did say he "would speak about it later when he was convinced that we knew enough algebra to appreciate it." This reporter guesses that each row is a set of numbers that has some significance somewhere in some topic of algebra, whatever that is!

Documents Reveal Last Scientist to Work at the Library of Alexandria

Newly discovered documents reveal that the last scientist to work at the 700-year-old Library of Alexandria was a mathematician and physicist by the name of Hypathia. She was also an astronomer and head of the Neoplatonic School of Philosophy. Her accomplishments were many in these important and (relatively) young areas of science. She died in C.E. 415, and shortly after her death, the library was deliberately burned to the ground, leaving only the remnants of the many thousands of its books.

Fibonacci Sequence Observed in Nature

A well-known pattern of numbers known as a *Fibonacci sequence* starts with 1,1 and adds the two terms. Each new number is added

---

Fibonacci Exercise

Fill out a few more terms of the Fibonacci Sequence and look up where in nature other such patterns appear.

---

to the number that immediately precedes it, thus, 1, 1, 2, 3, 5, 8, . . .

This sequence is observed in nature. For instance, the number of spirals on a pine cone fits this pattern. "But this is not all," claims Dr. Carla Vanetta, professor of mathematics at the University of Pisa. "This pattern keeps appearing and reappearing throughout nature, particularly in the life sciences.

Quite a mystery!"

Eratosthenes of Ancient Greece Found to Have Estimated the Size of Earth

The Greek philosopher and scientist Eratosthenes measured Earth around 235–240 B.C.E. He compared the length of a shadow cast by a tall tower in Alexandria with that of the shadow cast in Syene 500 miles south of Alexandria at exactly 12 noon. "Actually," admits Professor Celeste DeGloria, professor of astronomy at the University of Pisa, "he used a deep water well in Syene known to reflect the sunlight at exactly noon on one day, namely June 22, meaning that the sun was directly overhead at that time on that date.

The next year at that time on the same date he made a measurement of the length of a shadow made by a tall obelisk in Alexandria. This meant that in Syene no shadow would be cast by the sun directly overhead but a shadow would be cast in Alexandria, some distance away, thus indicating Earth must be curved." She continued to explain that a few simple calculations from geometry, using ratios, could reveal the radius of Earth. "It is truly remarkable," says Giovanni Guzzi, student of Professor DeGloria, "that his calculations were very close, in fact within 5 percent of what we know to be the true radius of Earth!"

Mind Teaser

Where on Earth would there be no shadow cast at 12 noon?

Where on Earth would the longest shadow be cast at 12 noon?

Earth Measurement Exercise

At 12 noon on any day, put a small stick vertically into the ground and observe its shadow. Note the approximate direction the shadow points (N, S, E, or W) in your laboratory notebook. Every hour, record the new position of the shadow and the time in your notebook. Measure the angles of the shadows using a small drawing protractor marked in degrees, and compare the measurements.

THE TELESCOPE,
Principal Instrument at the Core of Galileo's Work

In support of the Copernican worldview, in which the Sun is the center of all planetary motion rather than the earth, Galileo proposes an incredible finding. In recent observations of the planet Jupiter through the newly (Dutch) invented telescope, Galileo reports observing four small minor planets, he calls moons or satellites, revolving around the planet, "if the earth is the center of all planetary motion, then apparently no one was kind enough to inform these little moons that they had mistaken Jupiter for the earth !" reports Professor Galilei.

"Certainly, this must convince all of those who doubt the Copernican theory, that the earth is not the center of all motion" said by Antonio Vivace, friend and neighbor to Professor Galilei, "I've seen them myself, . . . why just last evening !" he says.

But not all are convinced, as Galileo says, "In a letter I recently wrote to the great Kepler, I mentioned that a colleague and friend, at the University of Padua, wouldn't even look through my telescope, and he even teaches philosophy." "I must admit, he continues, "that this convinces me that Copernicus was right, the Sun, rather than the earth, is the center of all planetary motion we observe."

Kepler's Third Law Exercise
Look up Kepler's third law and write it in your laboratory book. Include drawings, numbers, and anything else you need to remember it fully and accurately.

Kepler Reports Consistency with Galileo's Observations of Jupiter

In a surprise news conference, Johannes Kepler, assistant to the famous Tycho Brahe, announces that recent "moons of Jupiter" data, sent to him by Professor Galileo, fit extremely closely to his 3rd law. "I used Professor Galilei's data for the distances of the Jovian moons and their respective periods of revolution around Jupiter and find incredible agreement with my already established 3rd Law for the planets revolving around the Sun." He exclaims, "I'm amazed, at the consistency of our results and I now suppose the hunt is on to explain what is really going on." "It is truly an exciting time to be alive !" he concludes.

Notes

Your students will have a blast increasing their logical-mathematical intelligence!

A MATHEMATICAL MYSTERY TOUR
Higher-Thinking Math Tasks
By Mark Wahl
Grades 5–12

Now you can integrate math into art, science, philosophy, history, social studies, and language arts. Students solve problems, make inferences, formulate results, visualize, and have fun while using higher-thinking skills.

The required *Mystery Tour Guide* newspaper works well with each unit, adding questions, activities, puzzles, and tidbits of mathematical information. You'll receive a sample newspaper with the purchase of each book. Order additional newspapers in sets of five. Students should have their own newspapers, or if funds are limited, 3–4 students can share.

A Mathematical Mystery Tour (Book)
256 pages, 8½" x 11", softbound;
with sample newspaper

1006-W . . . $35

Mystery Tour Guide Newspaper
Please Note: This follow-along newspaper accompanies the book. One copy is recommended for each participant.
16 page tabloid, 11" x 17"

Set of Five Newspapers—1007-W . . . $9.95

ORDER FORM ☎ Please include your phone number in case we have questions about your order.

Qty.	Item #	Title	Unit Price	Total
	1006-W	A Mathematical Mystery Tour	$35	
	1007-W	Mystery Tour Guide Newspaper	$9.95	

Name _____

Address _____

City _____

State _____ Zip _____

Phone (_____) _____

Method of payment (check one):

❑ Check or Money Order ❑ Visa

❑ MasterCard ❑ Purchase Order attached

Credit Card No. _____

Expires _____

Signature _____

Subtotal	
Sales Tax (AZ residents, 5%)	
S & H (10% of Subtotal-min $3.00)	
Total (U.S. Funds only)	

CANADA: add 22% for S& H and G.S.T.

100% SATISFACTION GUARANTEE

Upon receiving your order you'll have 90 days of risk-free evaluation. If you are not 100% satisfied, return your order in saleable condition within 90 days for a 100% refund of the purchase price. No questions asked!

Call, Write, or FAX for your FREE Catalog!

Zephyr Press®
REACHING THEIR HIGHEST POTENTIAL

P.O. Box 66006-W
Tucson, AZ 85728-6006

(520) 322-5090
FAX (520) 323-9402